Metaphor in Psychotherapy

Publisher's Note

This publication is designed to provide accurate and authoritative information in regard to the subject matter covered. It is sold with the understanding that the publisher is not engaged in rendering psychological, medical or other professional service.

Books in "The Practical Therapist Series" present authoritative answers to the question, "what-do-I-do-now-and-how-do-I-do-it?" in the practice of psychotherapy, bringing the wisdom and experience of expert mentors to the practicing therapist. A book, however, is no substitute for thorough professional training and adherence to ethical and legal standards. At minimum:

- *The practitioner must be qualified to practice psychotherapy.*
- *Clients participate in psychotherapy only with informed consent.*
- *The practitioner must not "guarantee" a specific outcome.*

— Robert E. Alberti, Ph.D.

Metaphor in Psychotherapy

Clinical Applications of Stories and Allegories

Henry T. Close, Th.M.

The Practical Therapist Series™

Impact Publishers®

SAN LUIS OBISPO, CALIFORNIA 93406

Impact Publishers and colophon are registered trademarks of Impact Publishers, Inc.

ATTENTION ORGANIZATIONS AND CORPORATIONS:
This book is available at quantity discounts on bulk purchases for educational, business, or sales promotional use. For further information, please contact Impact Publishers, P.O. Box 910, San Luis Obispo, CA 93406-0910 (Phone: 1-800-246-7228).

Library of Congress Cataloging-in-Publication Data

Close, Henry T.
    Metaphor in psychotherapy : clinical applications of stories and allegories / Henry T. Close.
        p.   cm. -- (The practical therapist series)
    Includes bibliographical references and index.
    ISBN 1-886230-10-2 (alk. paper)
    1. Metaphor -- Therapeutic use.   2. Psychotherapy.   3. Storytelling--
Therapeutic use.   I. Title.   II. Series.
RC489.M47C58   1998
616.89'14--dc21   98.7500
                                            CIP

Cover design by Sharon Schnare, San Luis Obispo, California
Printed in the United States of America on acid-free paper
Published by **Impact ✆ Publishers®**
POST OFFICE BOX 910
SAN LUIS OBISPO, CALIFORNIA 93406-0910

Dedication

*This book is dedicated
with affection and respect
to my friend and colleague
Burrell Dinkins*

Appreciation

Thanks to the many people who have influenced me over the years. Since for the most part, I do not remember who taught me what, my gratitude is generic rather than specific. Though my two best-known teachers were Milton Erickson and Carl Whitaker, I have also studied with Stephen Lankton, John Warkentin, Fritz Perls and many others.

I especially appreciate the friends who have encouraged me — sometimes pushed me — in the writing of this book: Burrell Dinkins, Jenny Felder, Jeffrey Zeig, Florence Kaslow. Warm thanks to all of you.

Special thanks to my editor Bob Alberti, whose patience and wisdom were especially helpful to me.

Thanks also to you, my clients, for letting me be part of your lives for a while. Thank you for inviting me to be open with you, and for pushing some of my own growing edges. Thank you for stimulating my own creativity and nurturing.

I take very seriously the matter of confidentiality, and have made every effort to protect your identity. Many times, I think even you would not recognize you. Many of the people I have identified as male were in reality female, and vice versa.

In reporting my own comments, I have often written what I *wish* I had said, rather than what I actually said. My purpose in this book is to present the very best I have to offer, not to portray my inadequacies.

Contents

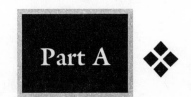

Part A

Introduction

Introduction

When I read books on psychotherapy, I usually read the first few pages dutifully. Typically, these are pages that develop the theoretical underpinnings of the book. But soon I find myself thumbing through the rest of the book to try to find some clinical vignettes, which I then read with relish.

For a long time, I attributed this to my being kind of flaky and easily bored. But then I began to wonder if there might not be some kind of inner wisdom behind this: the stories were more important, and I was impatient to get on with them!

I would eventually read all the theory parts and try to incorporate some of that into my work. But if I can respond to the charm of the stories, I am drawn into the heart of a book. I then tend to approach my clients with greater warmth and wisdom.

We now understand that stories address a different part of the psyche — perhaps even a different part of the brain — than is addressed by logic and explanation. It is this part of the psyche that is the primary source of animation, change and growth. This book is about approaches to psychotherapy that stem from this part of the psyche — the heart.

In the early 1950s, Carl Whitaker headed the department of psychiatry at Emory University in Atlanta. He wanted to teach psychiatry to the medical students experientially rather than academically. So he had all the first-year medical students in group therapy. The second-year students saw patients under close supervision. Only in the third year did they receive lectures in psychiatry. This book is somewhat similar. The many stories and vignettes throughout the book are the experiential background. The more theoretical chapters seek to place this experiential material in a coherent framework.

When I was in training, some 2½ paradigms ago, much therapy had a masculine quality to it. It tended to be highly confrontational. Therapeutic comments were often pithy one-liners, sometimes obscure, often obscene, with a kind of intrusive quality.

The approach of this book is more feminine in nature. Comments from this perspective tend to be much more elaborate, graceful, gentle. I agree with Milton Erickson, who said that therapy should above all else be charming!

In a typical book targeted at the "mind," the author will present a carefully reasoned process of logic, with appropriate illustrations. *This is how learning takes place at this (cognitive) level.* In a book oriented to the heart, the author will want to saturate your mind with examples of therapeutic interventions: stories, meditations, and suggestions. *This is how learning takes place at this (affective) level.*

It was much easier and more fun for me to write the stories than the theory. The stories came easily, perhaps because they involved memories of people who have been important to me. I am convinced that it is the stories that lead to change, not only in the lives of our clients, but also in our own approaches to therapy.

There seem to be several dichotomies implicit in much contemporary therapy: thinking/feeling; being/doing; authenticity/manipulation. This book is necessarily dualistic also. What matters is the interplay between polarities, the balance between one mode of functioning and another: the heart and the mind; the realistic and the worthwhile; the directions and the energy.

❖   ❖   ❖   ❖   ❖

I am a pastoral counselor by profession, as well as a marriage and family therapist. I think training in ministry is an excellent background for any therapist. Religion is primarily oriented to the heart, and the historic languages of religion are the languages of the heart.

The basic logic of this book is that people's difficulties in life result from world views that are deficient or distorted. We have acquired those world views indirectly, as by-products of living, rather than logically, by exhortation and reason. For example, I become anxious when I feel threatened. That is not the result of logical analysis. It stems from my experiences in living.

I may get defensive when I am insulted. That reaction too reveals from a particular world view: "People should think I am wonderful!" This is not a logical deduction, but an expression of the complex pathologies of my growing up.

The "languages" which build our world view are *drama* (the myriad experiences of living), *metaphor* (family stories), *fantasy* (the products of our imagination), and *ritual* and *ceremony* (special activities that define ultimate values).

These are "languages of the heart" and are associated with the right hemisphere of the brain.

From this perspective, *therapy consists of helping people change their world views. This is done most effectively by using the same languages which created the world views in the first place: drama, metaphor, fantasy, ritual and ceremony.*

Most of us know these things intuitively. I hope this book will — among other things — help you listen to and appreciate these languages of the heart.

2

A Boy and His Kite
An Allegory on Intimate Relationships

There was once a very unusual kite named Nancy. You may think it strange that this kite had a name. Few kites do. That is unfortunate. Every kite deserves a name. It is part of a kite's personality, its soul.

Anyone who has ever flown a kite knows that every kite has a *mind* of its own. But it is not always clear that it also has a *heart* of its own, a soul of its own. Part of the reason for this is that the heart — the soul — of a kite seldom gets cultivated. It is seldom encouraged to come into its own and blossom forth in its full beauty. It takes time for a heart to unfold itself to the world, and you just can't rush it.

When you buy a kite in a store, it is all rolled up compactly. For it to take shape, you have to unroll it, readjust its structure and bend it some (but you mustn't bend it too far or too quickly). Then you tie it together here and there, sometimes adding a tail for stability. Then it looks like a kite.

7

This is what you have to do to the *heart* of the kite also. In its own way, it needs to be carefully unrolled and stretched out. It needs to have its structure adjusted, bent a little — but not too much — a heart doesn't unfold itself in the presence of impatience. And ties need to be established.

Most of the time, unfortunately, a kite doesn't get this kind of attention. Many kites therefore never develop a soul. If a boy hurriedly buys a kite in a store, throws it together hastily to use for an afternoon in the wind before discarding it, there is no interest in cultivating its soul.

It turns out that most kites are treated just like that. They have been purchased in a store and never had their souls developed. Nobody bothers to give them names.

But if a boy *makes* his kite, that is a different matter. And Nancy was very much a homemade kite. The boy who had created her had seen a picture in a magazine of a beautiful kite. He was determined to have one like it for his very own. So he drew the design as well as he could from the picture, bought some good materials and joyfully went to work.

He talked to his kite while he made her — that is essential if the kite is to have much of a soul. A kite is very much like a person in that regard — it never really blossoms unless it is talked to. He would say things like, "Nancy, you are going to be a beautiful kite," or, "Look how lovely your arms look extended like that," or, "You're my very own kite, Nancy, and I want you to be very special."

He called her Nancy from the very beginning, although he didn't know anyone named Nancy. I don't even know how he knew to give her a girl's name instead of a boy's name, except that most kites that have names have girls' names. Maybe girls' kites have boys' names. I don't know. You would have to ask the girls and boys who make them — or maybe the birds that fly in the wind among the kites. As for Nancy, she loved her name, and she loved to hear him say it when he talked to her.

Finally the work was done, and he held her up to admire her. She looked something like a long slender bird, with graceful wings extended. He was very pleased and jumped up and down with excitement. He could hardly wait until the weekend when he could take her to an open field and fly her.

When Saturday came and he drove with his father into the country, he thought of some of the other kites he had made. For as long as he could remember, he had wanted a kite that would be unique, something set apart from all the other kites in the world. He had thought at first of trying to build the largest kite ever built. But when he started reading about kites, he realized that this would be impossible. People before him had built kites that were really enormous. Many of them had to be anchored to the earth with steel cables on power-driven winches.

He then thought of making the smallest kite in the world. He even tried this once, ending up with a tiny sliver of a thing that was just under an inch long. But this felt grotesque to him. It wasn't really a kite; it was just an oddity. He threw it away before even trying to fly it.

The uniqueness he sought would have to come from a different source.

It had taken him a long time to get the hang of making a kite that was really satisfactory. Most of them hadn't lasted very long. A string would break, or a gust of wind would catch one and throw it in a nosedive into a tree, or it would get caught on something.

Once he had let out every bit of string when a strong gust of wind caught the kite. Down it flew. He ran downwind as fast as he could, hoping to slow its fall, but he couldn't run fast enough. Finally he had to choose. Would he hold on to the string and hope that at the last second the wind would let up? Or would he let go of the string and lose the kite altogether? He chose to hold on and felt a little guilty when it plunged into a scrubby tree.

No, none of his other kites had had names.

He didn't like it if a kite was either too stable or too unstable. It scared him if a kite immediately started bolting hither and yon as soon as it was airborne. He would want to pull it in right away and add more tail. But if it was too stable, it didn't seem alive. It was just there, with him holding a lifeless string. There was no real sense of interaction.

He really liked it when Dad or another friend would hold the string at one end while he walked the kite out as far as he could downwind — to the very end of the string, if possible. When a little puff of wind came, he would hold her up as high as he could and then let go, to watch her ascend.

He also liked to take a kite down the same way. He would protect his hand from burning by putting a handkerchief around the string. Then he would walk toward the kite, thereby pulling her to earth — bucking, resisting, straining, like a petulant child being taken to bed.

For Nancy's first flight, they went to a nearby lake shore where several large fingers of land jutted out into the water. When the wind blew down the length of the lake and across this point, it was smooth and consistent — an ideal place for the trial flight of a very special kite. The wind was gentle that day, as if to help.

Nancy took to the air like a bird. Her movements were not jerky and irregular, but smooth and graceful. She would move to one side and then the other, occasionally swooping down as if playfully thanking him for letting her be there. He sometimes ran back and forth across the point of land, waiting for her to follow him. Or he would run forward a few steps and stop suddenly, looking up to watch the bend of the string travel slowly up to the kite.

Finally he lay down on a grassy patch where he could look up into the sky. With his head turned a little to the right, his field of vision included the tops of some of the tall poplar trees growing nearby. They were his point of reference, and the clouds moved by in relation to the trees.

But if he stared at the clouds for a while, *they* became his point of reference. For a few moments, it felt as though the clouds were stationary as he fixed his eyes on them. It was the trees that seemed to move, and the earth he was lying on felt like it was tilting backwards. He loved losing his sense of equilibrium this way.

He found he could do the same thing if he stared at his kite. When the wind was very steady for a period of time, so the kite was moving slowly and gently, the kite herself would become the reference point. Everything else seemed to move in relation to her. He could feel the earth sway beneath him. Even the clouds moved erratically back and forth relative to her.

For those moments, she had become the fixed point in his world, the center. He could surrender his sense of orientation to her and be caught up in the ecstasy of feeling a whole new orientation to his world.

In other words, she had become unique. Her uniqueness had nothing to do with how big or how small she was, or even how pretty she was or how different she was from other kites. No, it had to do with his relationship to her, his sense of experiencing his world differently because of her, with her as the reference point.

Anyone who has ever loved will recognize that this is what it is to be in love. A person is unique because you love her, not the other way around. This phenomenon is present in other relationships as well and, of course, it is the essence of what it means to be a believer.

Although the boy was not old enough or wise enough to express it this way, or even to think of it this way, this is what he felt. He experienced his world differently because of her; he felt the power of her uniqueness. He loved her.

H. Close, "A boy and his kite," originally published in *Voices: The Art and Science of Psychotherapy,* Summer, 1979. Adapted with permission of the publisher.

    I wrote this story as a wedding present for my wife, Nancy. I have given it to people concerned about the nature of intimacy (including couples who are getting married). I have also given it to a few middle-aged women who were concerned about no longer being "beautiful."

Part B

Metaphor

3 ❖

Metaphor

All sorrows can be borne if you put them into
a story or tell a story about them.
— Isak Dinesen

E ven after many years of telling stories to clients, I am still often surprised by their power to communicate.

One day, a client I had seen only a few times told me with considerable embarrassment about a terribly painful part of her history. I responded with a kind of personal metaphor: "What I think of is a time in my own life when . . . " I then described a related incident in my life, and how reluctant I was to tell anyone about it. She looked at me with tears in her eyes and said, "You really know how I feel."

With another client, I summarized an allegory about dependency and separation (*The Potted Tree,* chapter 15). Susan told me she never realized a man could understand the kinds of things she was struggling with.

Howard put it this way, "When you tell me these stories, what you are saying is that you really care about what happens to me."

15

Roxanne asked me somewhat playfully, "Did you make up that story just for me? Did you stay up all night just to make up that story to tell me today?" On another occasion, she told me, "When I tell you something, you don't just *tell* me you understand. You tell me some story, and then I *know* you understand, and that you're not laughing at me."

This kind of thing has happened with my clients many times over the years. Stories address a different level of consciousness than conceptual replies. They elicit a different level of response. Stories tend to be more believable than "objective" statements. A brilliant comment is what the therapist is "supposed" to say. A metaphor is not presented as something to be evaluated, but rather as a work of art. It is to be enjoyed and experienced on the basis of its own criteria.

Metaphors have impressive staying power. I saw a very depressed woman once on an emergency basis when her therapist was on vacation. As part of my support of her, I told her the story about the tree in winter (near the end of chapter 19). Three years later, I saw her in the waiting room. When I finally figured out who she was, I asked her how she was doing. She told me it was still winter.

When I think back on my own therapy, it is the stories my therapist told me that I remember, not his theories or explanations. On one occasion, Carl (Whitaker) told me about a dream he had when he was in therapy. In his dream, he was very small. He crawled up under his therapist's sweater, curled up next to his heart, and went to sleep. He then said that as far as he knew, he was still there; he had never crawled out.

Carl could have simply told me that positive transference was all right. I might have remembered that for the rest of the day. But the metaphor has stayed with me for years. I can't imagine ever forgetting it or the feelings of tenderness and warmth that accompany it.

I've told this story many times in seminars and workshops. Almost always, a number of people will remember fondly incidents from their own therapy. That, too, is one of the values of metaphor. It stimulates one's own memories of similar kinds of experiences. If I tell you about my children, you are likely to think of experiences with your children. I may talk about what it was like for me to grow up as a functional only child. That can easily stimulate reflections about the sibling configuration you grew up with, and how that may have affected you.

There is a quality of graciousness in the use of metaphor that tends to by-pass power struggles. Metaphor *invites* you to embrace its truth; logic is more demanding. Logic is generally associated with authority. As such, it elicits either resistance or a kind of passive acquiescence.

Metaphor invites you into its world, to identify with the story or with the teller. It invites you to partake of its world view and to try out that world view in your own fantasy. Metaphor does not lead to conclusions, but to different perspectives on situations. A given story may have different meanings for different people.

Jay Haley told of sending a group of his students to see Milton Erickson. When they returned, one student was particularly touched at Erickson's sensitivity to his own issues. The student then related one of the stories that Erickson had told the group. He said he knew this story was intended specifically for him.

Another student corrected him, and said that story was for *her*, not for him. She pointed out a few of its features that addressed her issues.

Haley said he found that very strange. He had heard that same story years earlier and knew that Erickson had created it specifically for *him*!

❖   ❖   ❖   ❖   ❖

There is much emotional processing that can take place *without* cognitive awareness. Much (most?) of our learning and growth takes place at an unconscious level. The things that stimulate those processes — like metaphor — have a tremendous power. They are like seeds that are planted in the subconscious mind. Those that find fertile ground will take root and sprout; those that are not suited will simply fade away.

A well-known family therapist told me he had seen Milton Erickson for one session of hypnotherapy. He had no memory of anything Erickson said, but he was aware of some significant changes in his life over the next few years.

I saw a sensitive and idealistic woman who was in her forties when she married for the first time. Jim was a widower with two difficult teenage children. His work consumed most of his time, so he turned the full responsibility of his children over to Marian. Having had no children of her own, she of course made lots of mistakes. The kids resented her for everything she did to try to be a loving and responsible stepmother. So I told her a story.

People who train wild animals, such as lions, have suggested that animals in an unfamiliar situation (such as a cage) will back off from an intruder unless the intruder gets too close. Then they will attack. Successful trainers seem to have an incredible intuitive ability to walk right on this imaginary dividing line. The animal doesn't know whether to back off or to attack. The resulting confusion allows the animal to be trained. Along with this, of course, is a lot of bonding behavior on the part of the trainer, which is essential.

At one circus, the trainer hired an apprentice who knew absolutely nothing about the work. When she arrived, the trainer took her to meet the other circus people, and then to see the animals and the facilities. Two minutes before the first show that afternoon, the trainer was suddenly stricken with illness and could not perform. So the manager gave the whip and chair to the apprentice, shoved her into the cage with the two lions and told her to go to work.

When I told Marian this metaphor, she replied enthusiastically, "That's it. I'm in the cage with wild animals, and I haven't had the first lesson about how to deal with them."

Metaphor has not always been recognized as a legitimate language of psychotherapy. A workshop participant once told me, "This new approach, using right brain techniques and metaphor, is what I have been doing in my counseling for years. I just thought that I wasn't being very professional." Another therapist, who had read my article on metaphor, told me it was a great relief to know that what he had been doing for years was all right

Metaphor is employed in many ways in our culture. In Alcoholics Anonymous, for instance, people tell their stories. Other people identify with these stories, and in that

identification, find strength. Many articles are written about horrible things that people have endured — accidents, bereavements, illnesses, violence, injustice. Others obviously find consolation and strength in these stories — much more so than if some authority simply told them to be strong.

The most common use of metaphor is probably telling nursery stories to children as part of bedtime rituals. Whatever hassles have been part of the day are laid aside. The intimacy of storytelling creates the atmosphere for sleep. The dark room, the soft voice, the parent's time and attention set the stage. The characters and the situations in the stories then become part of the world view that is subtly created and enhanced.

When I tell a story to a client, I am sharing something of my own inner life. I am at least saying, "This is important to me. I am the kind of person who appreciates stories like this. I am sharing something of me with you." If the story is about me, that makes it even more personal.

I usually don't tell success stories about me. If I want to tell a success story, and it happens to be about me, I may describe it as being about a friend. (I do consider myself to be my own friend.)

Many of the stories I tell about me are about my own humanness (embarrassments, struggles, failures). I hope these can help other people to be more at ease with their humanness. Other stories about me may be of some of the ways I have parented my children. Maybe the client can let the child part of him/her be parented vicariously.

Mary Catherine Bateson wrote of the time she was undertaking an anthropological research project in Iran. This would require her and her family to live with an Iranian family for an extended length of time. She was concerned about how Vanni, her five-year-old daughter, would deal with all the cultural differences.

Several weeks before they left, she started telling Vanni a series of nursery stories about Stacy the cow. Stacy wanted to know how the other animals in the barnyard lived. She thought the best way to find this out would be to go and live with the other animals for a while. Every night, Mary Catherine would tell Vanni about another of Stacy's adventures.

First Stacy visited the chickens. She thought it was very strange that the chickens ate little grains of food from the ground. And she had a very hard time trying to sleep on the chicken roost. When Stacy visited the horses, she didn't know how they could ever understand each other. They didn't moo like cows did, but made strange neighing sounds. She couldn't understand why the pigs seemed to enjoy wallowing in the mud.

When the family got settled in Iran, and Vanni seemed to be troubled about some of the customs there, her mother would remind her of the trouble Stacy had understanding and adapting to the other animals. She felt that the metaphoric preparation made Vanni's adjustment much easier. (Bateson, M.C., 1984.)

When I was growing up in Miami in the 1930s, my mother served for a while on the Dade County Board of Education. She came home after one meeting and said that a new high school principal had been introduced to the Board, an African American who had just finished his Ph.D.

from Harvard and would be working at one of the then-black schools. In the board discussion that followed, my mother asked him a question, addressing him as "Dr. ___". He told her after the meeting that she was the first white person ever to address him as "Doctor."

I no longer believe this story; Mother had a way of exaggerating everything. But in a deeper sense, I do believe it, and know its truth. Mother was defining us as a family. She was saying to me, "This is the kind of family we are; this is the kind of persons we are." It is significant that I have remembered this incident after all these years. If Mother had simply instructed me to treat black people with the same courtesy that I treat white people, I might have incorporated some of that. But the instruction would have had none of the power of the metaphor.

The woman's name was Mary, her husband's name was Joseph, and they had a beautiful precocious two-year-old son. I had seen the couple a few times for marital concerns. A few days before Christmas, Mary came to our session in a panic: she was going to give birth to the Messiah on Christmas day (she was not pregnant)! After listening to her carefully, I told her she had a beautiful fantasy; her child was as important to her as Jesus was to God. That was a really beautiful fantasy.

As I said this, I could see the anxiety drain from her face. I do not know if this was an accurate interpretation. But the fact that I recognized it as a metaphor rather than as an objective reality gave her a great sense of peace.

Alysha was picked up by the police wandering the streets of Atlanta at four o'clock in the morning. She told them she had the power to make the sun rise in the north and set in the south. She also claimed the power to transfer a death. If a person were going to die before his/her time, she could take that death and transfer it to an animal. The animal would die instead of the person.

The police immediately took her to the psychiatric unit at the county hospital. She was pronounced schizophrenic and treated with heavy medication and shock treatments. Several months later, she began work with me.

After several sessions Alysha apparently felt she could trust me enough to tell me about the "bizarre" claims that led to her arrest and hospitalization. I told her I thought it was a wonderful fantasy. She wanted to bring about the dawning of a new day that would alleviate human suffering. That is a beautiful dream and a worthwhile goal. I just hoped she wouldn't take on too much responsibility in relation to the world or even in relation to her family.

She said she really appreciated that way of looking at it. She also bitterly resented the psychiatric unit for not understanding her. I reminded her that in her family of origin, she had been the caretaker and rescuer. It was certainly not surprising that she experienced things in such global terms.

A rather slight young man in his early 20s from a small town in rural Georgia, Ken was admitted to a mental health facility because of his bizarre religious ideation and occasional thoughts that he was God. We had talked together briefly several times prior to the following exchange in my office.

We were talking about God, and I commented that I thought of God as in some sense being with us as we talked.

Pointing to an empty chair, Ken asked, "Where, in that chair?"

"I think of God as kind of being everywhere, but would you rather picture God as being in that chair?"

"No, . . . I'd like for you to be in that chair, and you be God."

"O.K." (I moved to the empty chair.) "Now I'm God, and I'm here to be with you and to listen to you."

With that, he confessed to me that he had committed many sins. I told him that I knew he had done many things wrong and that he had made many mistakes. I wanted him to know that I wasn't out to get him. I forgave him for everything he had done wrong.

He then asked me how I and Jesus and the Holy Spirit all got along with each other. I took this to be a reference to his family, who didn't get along with each other. I told him we managed to resolve whatever differences we might have. These didn't interfere with our caring for him and listening to him.

He then knelt before me with his hands folded as in prayer and said he wanted to worship me. I placed my hands on his head and told him I was blessing him. He was my child. I loved him and I was blessing him.

When he got up and sat back in his chair, the encounter felt finished to me. I got back in my chair and asked him what it was like to have done that. He said it was great and he really felt better. As he left the office, he hugged me warmly and thanked me for the experience, assuring me that hugging did not imply homosexuality.

I experienced this encounter as very intimate and very significant. I made it a point to look him up on the ward that evening before I went home. He greeted me warmly, addressing me as "Chaplain Close," and thanked me again for the experience.[1]

I noticed one day in the spring that all the trees around my office were in bloom except for a magnificent big hickory tree. (I did not know at that time that trees of the walnut family are always the last to bloom in the spring.) Its limbs were bare, and it looked stark and dead. As I looked closer, I noticed the first beginnings of some buds on the lower branches. On closer examination, I saw that there were new buds all over the tree.

It so happened that I was on my way to see a very depressed client who was struggling with a pervasive sense of hopelessness. She had arrived early, so I brought her out to the yard. From a distance I asked her to describe the tree. She, too, thought it was dead. I then took her closer and pointed out all the buds that were just beginning to appear. I did not interpret this, but merely said that I thought she would like to see the tree.

Several months later, in the autumn, she asked me if I had noticed the tree that was the late bloomer (I had not used this term). She said it had the most spectacular color of any tree in the yard, and against the electric blue of the sky it was magnificent!

A sanitation engineer spoke of the toxins that paper mills discharge into a river. If the river is in full flow, it can easily handle the waste material. It is converted by bacteria and plant life into harmless substances. But if the river flow is low, as in a prolonged dry season, the waste overwhelms the ability of the river to handle it. It can easily kill much of the life in the river. So it is essential to control the amount of waste discharged when the river flow is low.

I pointed out that this is true of marriages also. There is always toxic waste in a marriage. It can be handled only when there is a full flow of satisfactions. When the flow is low, one must make sure not to damage it with toxins.

A client said she had confided a lot of very personal material to a friend. A couple of weeks later, she was horrified to find out that the friend had gossiped about her to a mutual friend in a very condescending manner.

Bettie didn't know how to react to or deal with this situation. She couldn't confront her friend, because this would betray the person who told her. It would also end the relationship with the friend, who did not take confrontation gracefully! She thought of ending the relationship herself. But she didn't really want to do that, for in many ways she enjoyed this person. The most pressing question had to do with anger. Should she be angry at this friend. If so, what should she do with the anger?

I told Bettie, "When I lived in south Florida, I used to hike around in the forests that rim the Everglades. There are a lot of rattlesnakes in these forests — little pygmy rattlesnakes about two to three feet long. I don't remember ever being angry at the rattlesnakes for being there. Rattlesnakes are rattlesnakes, and that was where they lived. If I was going to walk through there, I was going to encounter them.

"But I didn't go barefoot! I wore heavy shoes and snake leggings, and watched where I stepped. But I wasn't angry at the rattlesnakes for being there."

At the end of the hour, Bettie told me she was going to get some heavy shoes and snake leggings. A few weeks later, she said she had had lunch with this friend. She remembered to wear snake leggings and had a very nice time.

---

[1]H. Close, "I Want You to be God, and I am Not God," originally published in *The Journal of Pastoral Care*, September, 1984, p. 243f. Adapted with permission of the publisher.

Therapeutic Metaphors for Children

Dr. Richard Gardner, a child psychiatrist in New York, has developed a wonderful technique for working with disturbed children, which he calls "The Mutual Storytelling Technique." Dr. Gardner tells his patient that all kids have many stories in their imagination. He then asks the child to make up a story to tell him. Dr. Gardner always comments approvingly on the child's effort.

He then makes up a story of his own, using the same characters and setting, but with an outcome that is healthier. I presume that when the child's stories no longer need improvement, he or she is cured.

Telling stories is a gentle and effective way to address children's issues. You offer them something that is enjoyable in its own right, that also has potential lessons. But if they wish, they can simply enjoy the story as an amusement.

Linda is a recently divorced mother in her middle twenties with a four-year-old son, Chris. Linda complained that Chris's behavior had suddenly taken a turn for the worse, especially when they were dining out. He does all right when they are eating out alone, or with one of her female friends. But when they eat out with her new boyfriend, Chris becomes fidgety, restless, and irritable.

I pointed out to Linda that the new boyfriend is a rival to Chris. I suggested that she might tell him some stories as a way to reassure him of his place in her life. Chris did not have any favorite animals (potential characters in a story), but he was very taken with heroes like Batman and Superman. I suggested the following story.

"Chris, did you know that Batman had a little boy? His name is Chrisboy. Sometimes Batman and Chrisboy will go out for supper together. Sometimes they go to McLizzard's or sometimes to the Snakeburger King, but their very favorite place to eat is Kansas Fried Worms. They will have a delicious dinner of lizard's feet, or bug burgers and French fried worms, and oh, that is *so* good!

"Sometimes they go with one of Batman's friends, like Frogman or Butterflyman, and Chrisboy really likes that. They talk with him and tell him all kinds of wonderful stories about their adventures. They all laugh together and have a wonderful time. But one day, Batman found himself a girlfriend named Kittenwoman and started spending more and more time with her.

"At first, Chrisboy kind of liked it that his Daddy had a girlfriend. She really liked him and told him stories, and she listened to everything he wanted to tell her. But after a while, Chrisboy didn't like Kittenwoman so much because Daddy was spending too much time with her. He would go out and spend a whole evening with her and leave Chrisboy alone with the babysitter, Bashful Bertha. Chrisboy didn't like that at all.

"So sometimes Batman would take Chrisboy with him when he went out for supper with Kittenwoman. For a while, Chrisboy would sit quietly, eating his delicious French fried worms and listening to Batman and Kittenwoman talk. But after a while, Chrisboy wanted them to pay more attention to him and talk to him instead of to each other. He didn't like it that his Daddy was giving so much attention to somebody else, no matter how nice she was.

"But Chrisboy was just a little boy, only four years old. He didn't know how to come right out and tell his Daddy, 'Daddy, I don't want you to give so much attention to somebody else. I want you to give more attention to me.' He just didn't know how to say that.

"Instead, he started squirming and fidgeting and fussing and whining. He put his feet up on the table and dropped his French fried worms on the floor. Daddy told him to be quiet and to sit up straight, but that made Chrisboy even more nervous and fidgety.

"When they got home that night, Batman told his little boy, 'Chrisboy, you were really fussy tonight at Kansas Fried Worms. You wouldn't sit still, and I was beginning to get a little bit irritated at you. I don't want to be irritated at you, but I don't understand why you were so fussy.'

"Chrisboy got kind of nervous when Daddy asked him that. He had never just told Daddy when something was bothering him, but now Daddy was asking him to do just that. So he looked at Daddy and said real quietly, 'I don't like Kittenwoman any more.'

"Well, Batman understood immediately what was going on.

" 'You don't like it when I talk too much to Kittenwoman and not enough to you?'

Chrisboy nodded.

" 'And you don't like it when Kittenwoman and I talk about things that you don't understand, and you feel left out?'

Chrisboy nodded again.

" 'And you don't like it when Kittenwoman and I laugh about things and you don't even know what we are laughing about? Do you feel like you're not important?'

Chrisboy nodded and started to cry just a little bit.

"So Batman hugged his little boy and told him he loved him very much. He would always love him. No one in the whole world would ever be as important to him as his little boy. He was sorry he had forgotten about that when they were eating out with Kittenwoman. The next time they all went out together for supper, he and Kittenwoman would both remember how important Chrisboy is to both of them.

"Chrisboy felt much better when his Daddy said that and hugged him very tight. And Batman hugged his little boy and told him, 'I'll always love you.'

Chrisboy told his Daddy, 'I'll always love you.'

"And that is the story of Batman and Kittenwoman and Chrisboy."

When I saw Linda again, she said Chris really liked the stories she was telling him.

A colleague who does not work with children referred the five-year-old daughter of one of her clients. Debbie came in with her mother for one session after the father had walked out on the family. The daughter had gone on a hunger strike, saying she wouldn't eat anything until her daddy came back home. This was particularly distressing to the mother, who was obsessed with food.

I found out as much as I could in the first third of the hour. I then told a long story about a family of cats (she had a pet kitten). The daddy cat left the family, and the kittens were feeling and doing lots of different things to deal with Daddy's leaving.

One of the kittens had heard of another kitten who refused to eat anything because she was so angry (Debbie was not overtly angry, so I thought I might let her know in this indirect way that anger was appropriate).

This kitten thought she, too, would refuse to eat anything. But she really enjoyed certain foods — hamburger and fish and cheese. It seemed a shame to give up everything. Finally she thought she could let Mommy Cat and Daddy Cat know how unhappy she was if she simply refused to drink her milk! Ever!

Mommy Cat would be very worried. She would plead with her to drink her milk, but the little kitten would refuse.

At the end of the story, Debbie asked me several questions about the kittens and how they dealt with the situation. I don't think she would have ever asked these questions without the safety provided by the story. In my answers, I could support, reassure, and teach without stirring up her self-consciousness and resistance.

A few weeks later, the mother reported that Debbie was eating normally, except for her refusal to drink milk.[1]

---

[1]H. Close, "Metaphor in Pastoral Care," originally published in The *Journal of Pastoral Care*, December, 1984, p. 302f. Adapted with permission of the publisher.

5

The Slimy Green Monster
A Story Addressing Children's Phobias

Children's stories can be wonderful opportunities for pediatric psychotherapy. As a pastoral counselor, I sometimes lead worship services and always enjoy including a sermon for the children.

On one occasion, I wanted to address their phobias — specifically their fear of monsters. These fears are distressing not only to the kids, but also to their parents, who are often unable to reassure the kids.

I think this kind of fear often results from an inner aggression that is disowned and then projected onto someone else. Therapy helps the child to reclaim the aggression and to incorporate it into his or her own psyche. But the child must feel that it is safe to do so. So I told the following story as part of a worship service.

Sitting on the floor with the kids, I leaned toward them, and spoke in a slow, deep, scary voice. "Once upon a time, there was a great . . . big . . . terrible . . . horrible . . . slimy green monster who liked to scare little children."

The five-year-old girl sitting next to me was obviously alarmed. She put her hands over her ears and said, "Oh no!"

I continued in the same slow menacing voice. "And do you know what that great big . . . terrible . . . horrible monster's name was?"

"No."

I paused a moment, sat up straight, smiled playfully and said cheerfully, "It was Jimmy, Jimmy J. Monster!"

They all giggled. I continued playfully.

"Sometimes Jimmy J. Monster would crawl under the children's bed at night. Then when they were fast asleep, he would crawl out and make terrible scary sounds. He would get right up next to their ears and would roar in their ears. But he said it very softly, like, 'roar.'

"Do you know why he whispered it so softly? One time he yelled out real loud and scary, 'ROAR!' But he said it so loud that he scared himself! He ran all the way home to his mommy and got up in her lap.

"She put her arms around him to tell him it was all right. She would protect him from that big bad noise. He was still her little baby — even though everybody else thought he was a great big, terrible monster. So he never said 'roar' again very loud, because he didn't want to scare himself again.

"You see, his mommy did not know that her little Jimmy went around at night trying to scare little children. She thought he was a very nice monster. When he went out at night, she thought he was just playing with his other monster friends, the slimy blue monster, and the slimy pink monster, and the slimy purple monster. That's what his mommy thought. She did not know that he was actually out trying to scare little children!

"One night, Jimmy came to a house in a big city, hoping to scare all of the children: the youngest one first, then the middle child, then the oldest. All three of them the very same night! That Jimmy J. Monster was really a mean monster.

"But do you know what happened? When Jimmy Monster crawled under the littlest boy's bed, his lollipop fell out of his pocket. It was a great big green lollipop, all wrapped up in pink paper. When the littlest boy climbed into bed, he saw the lollipop lying on the floor and knew exactly what it meant. He knew there was a slimy green monster under his bed.

"So he called his mommy, 'Mommy, there's a slimy green monster under my bed, that's going to try to scare me tonight.'

"Mommy came into the room and saw the green lollipop on the floor. She lifted up the edge of the covers and yelled at that monster. 'You listen to me, you big, slimy green monster. You're a bad monster to try to scare my children. If you ever come here again, I'm going to tell your mommy on you. You'll be in big trouble then. She won't let you watch cartoons for a whole week! So don't you ever come back here again, or you'll be in really big trouble!'

"Jimmy J. Monster didn't like that. He didn't like to be yelled at — monsters never like it when people yell at them. And he certainly didn't want his mommy to know that he had been trying to scare little children.

"He crawled out from under that bed just as fast as he could. He told the littlest boy's mommy, 'Oh please don't tell my mommy on me. I promise I'll never come here again. I'll do anything you want if only you won't tell my mommy on me.' With that, the littlest boy himself yelled at Jimmy J. Monster. 'You get out of here, you slimy green monster, and don't you ever come back.' "

At this point I asked the kids if they could demonstrate how they might yell at a monster, and I heartily approved of their performances before continuing.

"Well, Jimmy Monster ran away from there just as fast as he could, all the way home. He ran into his bedroom, closed the door, crawled into bed and pulled the covers over his head. He did not want anybody ever to yell at him again. And he sure didn't want to miss out on a whole week of watching cartoons.

"He thought and thought and thought for a long time. Finally he said to himself, 'I've got to figure out some other ways to have fun at night. What can I do when my friends are asleep, and I want to go out and have some fun?' Then he had an idea. He could go out at night and have a wonderful time *protecting* the little children.

"So whenever a little boy or a little girl thinks there is a great big, slimy green monster behind a tree at night, they can be very glad to know that the monster is there to protect them.

"Now, there is one more thing I haven't told you yet. It's about the lollipop that fell out of Jimmy J. Monster's pocket. The next morning, when the littlest boy woke up, he found the lollipop lying there, on the floor. The monster hadn't even unwrapped it yet. So he took the lollipop and put it on his dresser, on a little stand. Whenever he looked at it, he would laugh and laugh and laugh.

"And that is the story of the slimy, green monster and the littlest boy and the lollipop."

I then asked the kids, "So, do you know what to do if you ever think there's a monster in your room, trying to scare you?"

The little girl who had been so alarmed at the beginning mumbled something.

"What?" I asked.

"Kick his butt."

"Kick his butt! That's a great idea. You could kick his butt, or you could yell at him, or you could get Mommy and Daddy to yell at him too. Because no monster ever wants to be yelled at, and no monster every wants to get in trouble with his mommy."

There are three important principles implicit in this story. First, I needed to establish rapport. I knew all the kids, at least slightly, and liked them. I sat on the floor with them. To make contact with their fears, I started talking in a very scary voice.

Then I quickly reframed the whole situation. My tone of voice changed. I gave the monster a harmless sounding name and described him as non-dangerous. It is rather hard to be terrified of a monster who still sits in his mommy's lap so she can protect him. Or a monster who is terrified of being yelled at, who watches cartoons, and eats lollipops.

This was all expressed metaphorically, with the metaphor's inherent power to draw people into its world view. The effectiveness of this process was dramatically demonstrated by the little girl who had been so alarmed at the beginning. After hearing the story, she could envision herself displaying enough aggression to "kick his butt!"

6

The Flower Girl

I recently performed a wedding for two friends. At the rehearsal, the six-year-old flower girl was obviously unhappy. Her mother was insisting she march down the aisle properly, strewing petals. The girl was equally insistent that she would have no part of it. She was squirming, balking, fidgeting, while mother squeezed her arm and muttered threats under her breath. Finally she put the flower basket upside down on her head and walked down the aisle crying.

It was, nevertheless, important for the bride that her niece participate in the wedding. I wondered if I could do something that might help. I assumed that after being reprimanded and forced to do something she did not want to do, her self-esteem and her confidence were low. She needed affirmation. I thought of the value kids give to their names.

After the rehearsal I asked her her name.

"Tiffany."

"Tiffany?" I said excitedly, "Your name really is Tiffany?"

My animation got her attention, and she nodded in agreement.

"Do you know who else is named Tiffany?"

She shook her head.

"Do you remember the story of Goldilocks and the three bears?"

She nodded.

"Do you know what the papa bear's name was?"

"No."

"It was Algonquin. Algonquin Bear. And do you know what the mama bear's name was?"

"No."

"It was Arabella. Arabella Bear. And do you know what the *baby* bear's name was? It was Tiffany! Tiffany Bear! And you have the same name as the Baby Bear!"

She was smiling by this time, and shook her head playfully.

"You do! I was talking with Goldilocks just the other day, and she told me the names of all three bears. Algonquin, Arabella, and Tiffany Bear.

"And did you know that Tiffany Bear was the flower girl in Goldilocks' wedding? [Once you get involved in telling a story, it is easy to get carried away!] She was! She walked right down the aisle and dropped those flower petals all the way. When Goldilocks walked down the aisl, she was so happy because her little friend Tiffany Bear had put those petals there for her to walk on. Goldilocks even winked at Tiffany as she was walking down the aisle.

"I think Goldilocks is going to be at this wedding tomorrow. And I think Mama Bear and Papa Bear will be here too. But I don't think Tiffany Bear will be here. She is visiting her grandmother. But you be sure to say 'hello' to Goldilocks and to Mama Bear and Papa Bear."

At the wedding, Tiffany performed beautifully. I would like to think my intervention contributed to that. After the wedding, I asked her if she had seen Goldilocks and the two bears. She assured me that she had, and we had a nice conversation about our "mutual friends."

I then told one of the older women what I had done with Tiffany. I asked her if she would go to Tiffany, identify herself as Goldilocks, and tell her how well she had done. The woman said she would, but I don't think she ever got around to it. Maybe that kind of thing is easier for those of us who are only part-time adults.

H. Close, "The Flower Girl," originally published in the *Newsletter of the Georgia Association for Marriage and Family Therapy,* 1992.

7

The Castle Beyond the Forest

The greatest barrier to the good is the search for perfection.

— Cardiologist Mark Cohen

Doris was approaching her sixty-fifth birthday and was still undecided about what to do with her life. Spiritually, she was a product of the human potential movement of the 1960s. She really bought into the emphasis on personal fulfillment and would settle for nothing less. The unhappiness she had seen in her mother underscored the importance of her ideals.

Although she had completed over eight years of college and graduate school, she still did not have a degree (the three graduate schools had accepted her provisionally). She would embark on a course of study with great enthusiasm but soon would lose interest. The material just did not hold her attention. So she would withdraw, only to begin another program in a different field within a year or two.

Her career path was similar. A many-talented woman, she had begun careers in a wide variety of fields: acting, writing, teaching and music (she could have been a successful performer as a singer, a pianist or a clarinetist). She had even considered a career in vocational counseling or as a family therapist. She would venture into one of these career paths with enthusiasm and resolve, confident that she could make a real contribution. But inevitably, her commitment would fade. That field simply did not offer the personal fulfillment she sought. Eventually, no field seemed worthy of her.

She was destined for greater things.

There had been a similar history of religious affiliation. She had at various times been passionately committed as a Methodist, Buddhist, Pentecostal, Atheist, Catholic and Unitarian. None offered her the depth of spirituality she regarded as indispensable.

After three years in college, she served two years in the Peace Corps. She had also lived in the inner city, suburbia, a commune that operated a farm, a high rise condo and an isolated mountain retreat.

Doris had never married. She had had a succession of wonderful relationships with really fine men, but no one ever seemed to meet her deeper needs. She knew she would be a wonderful partner if only she could find the right man.

In our work together (needless to say, I was but the latest in a long line of therapists), Doris and I often talked of her search for perfection — the Utopia Syndrome, as some have put it. On one occasion, I told her the following story.

Once upon a time there was a little girl who lived in the depths of an immense forest. She lived all alone, eating the nuts and berries that were within her reach, and sleeping under the canopy of leaves and branches, or in a hollowed-out place in the trunk of a great tree.

"The forest was dark and foreboding and frightening. Trees assumed grotesque shapes in the night, noises assailed her on all sides, and sometimes she could see the shapes of large animals as they appeared for a moment in a shaft of moonlight before disappearing into the shadows. Sometimes while she slept, it seemed that the vines would grow toward her in the night as though to wrap her in their tentacles to imprison her. Strangely enough, though, nothing in the forest had actually harmed her — not even a little bit. But the longer she travelled, the more ominous and frightening the forest became. It was almost as though it was determined to making her journey as difficult and arduous as possible.

"If she tried very hard, she could barely remember how she got in the forest, but that wasn't important to her now, so it isn't important to our story. What was important was her objective. For as long as she could remember, she had been told that at the far end of the forest, there was a beautiful castle rising from the rocky hillside, with golden tiles shimmering in the sun and alabaster walls exuding a radiance that surpassed all description.

"Inside the castle were the queen and king, eagerly waiting for her to come. Day after day, they would sit at the highest window or pace back and forth in front of the iron gate, looking forlornly into the forest, waiting just for her. They had a silk robe with glass slippers and a golden crown waiting for her, and at a moment's notice, the chef would begin the elaborate feast that would welcome her to the castle — to the place where she really belonged. Everything would be done to make up for the hardships of the journey.

"There was even a handsome prince who appeared every month at the time of the full moon, eager to bestow on her his undying love. The little girl dreamed of how she would be greeted and what she would say. She would comment on the dreams of the castle that gave her strength and determination, no matter how hard the journey or how discouraging the outlook. Day by day she trudged onward.

"Every once in a great while, she thought she could catch a glimpse of the castle in the distance, beckoning her onward, but for some days afterward, it seemed that the journey became even more full of peril and hardship.

"One day she happened to glance to her left and noticed that there was a clearing at the edge of the forest. Slowly she made her way through the thick underbrush to see what was there. To her astonishment, there was a modest field of wheat and in the distance, a crude cottage surrounded by fruit trees and a well-tended garden of vegetables and pretty flowers. She could see an elderly man and woman there, bent with age and hard work, obviously unsophisticated, but apparently kind and gentle.

"Coming down the road from the other side was a young man who seemed pleasant enough, but rather ordinary. He and the older couple greeted each other with what seemed to be genuine warmth. The sight of these people enjoying each other's company was very touching to the young girl, but she couldn't afford to spend too much time there watching, because her dreams of the castle with the king and queen and prince were beckoning her onward.

"Back she went into the forest, struggling through the undergrowth of vines and brambles and broken limbs and darkness and sinister sounds and shapes from the shadows.

"The next day, she crept again to the edge of the forest to look again at the rustic cabin and the people around it. She felt a strange attraction to them, which seemed bewildering to her. She knew she had been destined for greater things. She had been destined for royalty, to live in a castle where everything was wonderful. Quickly she turned away from the clearing and trudged once more into the depth of the forest.

"The next day she made her way again to the clearing. This time, the elderly man saw her and called to her. Very hesitantly she left the familiarity of the forest. She told the man and his wife about her dream of the castle and the queen and king who were waiting for her. The elderly couple said they, too, had heard of the magic castle and the royal couple who waited for the arrival of the princess. They shared their simple lunch with the girl and gave her a basket of bread and fruit to help her on her journey.

"That night she slept even more fitfully than before. The sounds of the animals seemed closer, more menacing. She thought about how often she had been terrified of these sounds, but that no harm had ever come to her. She began to wonder if their task was to frighten her rather than to harm her. But if this was the case, why???

"The next day, she went again to visit with the elderly couple and the young man. They made her feel so welcome and so comfortable that she lost track of the time. Finally, late in the afternoon, she realized that a whole day had passed without her gaining any ground in her pilgrimage to the castle. The elderly couple comforted her and insisted she spend the night with them.

"As she began to drop off to sleep, she contrasted in her mind the crude accommodations of this cottage with the luxury that awaited her at the castle. All night long, she dreamed of the castle and of her rightful place there. It became more real to her than it had ever been; in her mind, she could feel the softness of the sheets and clothing, and smell the fragrances from the garden and from the kitchen, and hear the beautiful music of the court musicians serenading her. It was truly wonderful.

"The next morning she awoke to the harsh realities of a very different world. There were chores to be done, tasks to be accomplished, and even then there was little leisure and none of the luxury she anticipated at the castle. After a quick breakfast, she ran to the forest to resume her journey.

"As she trudged through the dense undergrowth, she felt a strange attraction to the people she had left and to the lifestyle they enjoyed. She knew she was entitled to much better than that, but still, there was something appealing about its simplicity and its inherent goodness. Perhaps above all else, it was real.

"She had no doubt that the royal life of the castle really did exist, but deep down, she could not be sure. And even if it did exist, was it really there for her rather than for someone else? And what was she sacrificing in the process? The elderly couple has asked her to stay with them. They told her they would love her, which meant a lot to her. But she knew they could never give her the specialness to which she knew she was entitled.

"And then there were the two young men: the handsome prince who was waiting for her, and the simple country lad, good-natured and hard-working, but very ordinary. It grew more and more confusing for her. Her heart told her to follow her dream and let nothing deter her. But the dream became more and more elusive.

"Finally she made a very painful choice: she returned to the cottage. She chose the rather mundane realities of what was possible and gave up the vague unrealities of her dreams. After the first shock of disappointment had faded, she was quite surprised to find that she was actually happy. For a while, that bothered her, and she tried to suppress it. She told herself that she didn't deserve to be happy, since she had betrayed her dream. But then she would forget to hassle herself and came to feel a sense of belonging and well being. Eventually she and the young man were married and created a home of their own.

"Every once in a while, she would go to the forest just to experience being there. She no longer wished to pursue the dream, but the forest embodied a tremendous sense of energy and mystery and power that to her were very appealing. She would fight her way through the dense growth to a great log by a stream. There she would listen in awe and wonder to the sounds of the forest, shuddering a bit at the shadows and movements, feeling the musty air against her skin, and smelling the earthy fragrances of growth and decay and new life.

"It was only when her own daughter began to grow up, and there appeared a wistful, far-away look in her eye, that her mother told her about the castle and the forest and the king and queen who were probably still waiting for her to come, and how glad she was that she had chosen the life she had.

❖   ❖   ❖   ❖   ❖

Three years after our work together, Doris was working at a modest job and seemed relatively happy.

I gave this story once to a greatly admired university professor who was nearing retirement. His wife, also a distinguished professor, had died several years earlier. He was now dating a woman who would be a wonderful partner for him. But she had no academic credentials. He said he wanted someone just like her, but with a position comparable to his own. He wanted a wife who was his social equal.

In other words, he was looking for the castle beyond the forest.

He and the woman eventually married and seemed extremely happy together. I, of course, take total credit for their success.

H. Close. "The Castle Beyond the Forest," originally published in The Journal of Pastoral Care, Fall, 1996. Reprinted with permission of the publisher.

For Doris, with appreciation. When she read this chapter, she laughed at my exaggerations and said she remembered the story with warmth.

8

Painting Lessons

Helen had been sitting quietly on the couch for a long time, absorbed in her thoughts. This was not unusual. During the years I had known her, she was consistently silent during most of her therapy sessions. I had slowly learned how to respect that silence and how to support her rather than confront her.

I first saw Helen when she was a patient at the state mental hospital where I was chaplain. She had been admitted after three private hospitals had failed to help her. Helen had been sexually abused as a child but had managed to function until her middle teens. Then something triggered her memories, and she became seriously suicidal. On one occasion, an overdose of medication left her unconscious for three days.

I met Helen soon after her admission and began seeing her twice weekly for psychotherapy. I was dismayed when confronted by her silence. I had just finished my training and thought people needed to talk about their concerns if our time together was to be beneficial, so I tried the few techniques I had learned to get people to talk. Helen would respond to some of these, perhaps to keep me from feeling so totally incompetent.

One day, she commented on her silence.

"I'm aware I don't say much here in your office."

I acknowledged that.

"That doesn't mean I'm not getting anything out of these sessions. I can think thoughts here in your office I can't even think anywhere else. That's what's helping me get better."

Later, she told me that her other therapists had pushed her to talk. When she didn't, they grew impatient with her and diagnosed her as a hopeless case.

She was particularly angry at one well-known psychiatrist. He expected her to respond to his questions. From her point of view, that meant he had absolutely no understanding of her. He should have known she could not talk. And she certainly was not going to communicate with someone who did not bother to understand her. I seemed more willing to let her set her own pace and not insist that she talk.

At the time, I did not realize that I was being respectful of her silence. I just felt inadequate and incompetent because I did not know how to facilitate her talking.

As I reflect on that situation now, I think I understand it. When Helen would enter my office, she would immediately go into something like a hypnotic state. In that state, she could do the inner work necessary for her recovery. When I tried to get her to talk, I was calling her out of that inner state and thereby interfering with her therapy.

Eventually I learned to say only enough to support her in the inner processing she was doing.

Sometimes I would tell her a story.

❖   ❖   ❖   ❖   ❖

"There was once a young woman who had been given a beautiful painting of an adolescent girl, bright-eyed and eager as she faced her life and her thrilling future. But someone had defaced this picture. He had painted an evil horrible man in the background, with a gnarled ugly hand across the girl's face, obscuring her beauty and her pleasure in living.

"The young woman did not know what to do with this painting. It was certainly too ugly to let anyone see. She thought of throwing it away. Several times she actually took it out to the trash pile (this was a reference to the suicide attempts). Once she left it there for three days before retrieving it.

"On another occasion a friend found it on the trash pile with a couple of holes poked in it. She took it back to the young woman and suggested she take painting lessons.

"The young woman took this advice. She began to learn about colors and pigments and how to mix them to get the desired shades. She learned about brushes and strokes and how to move her hand. She learned about light and shadows and perspective and composition.

"When she felt she had learned enough, she took the troubling painting and began to study it very carefully. Her first reaction was disgust, and then a kind of fright. It would be easy to feel overwhelmed by the task that lay before her.

"But she persevered. She started by repairing the damage that the canvas had suffered on the trash pile. Next she bought some paint and brushes, and mixed the pigments very carefully. She then painted over the evil person and his ugly hand that obscured the face of the young girl.

"To her dismay, the dark pigments of this evil man started seeping through the new paint. Try as she might, she could not cover up that malignant influence.

"She was discouraged for a while but finally tried something else. Very carefully she took a razor blade (I deliberately mentioned a razor blade since she had used one to cut her wrists) and started scraping away the pigment that defined the ugliness.

"At first she scraped very tentatively, removing only the surface of the ugliness. But as time progressed, she scraped more confidently. Sometimes she would scrape away just a little bit and immediately fill in the area with new pigment to match the girl's skin. Sometimes she became impatient. She would scrape so vigorously that she actually removed some of the underlying pigment that defined the young girl. It left the painting marred and incomplete.

"On a couple of occasions, she scraped so hard that she tore the underlying canvas. But she was so pleased at being rid of the ugliness that she didn't mind the damage and the necessary repairs.

"She would then take her paints and brushes, mix the pigments carefully to get the desired colors and shades, and repaint the places that had been damaged.

"Finally she finished. Her skills as a painter were imperfect. The finished product did not look as beautiful as if it had not been damaged. Instead of a dream-like innocence, there was now a rugged, hardy feel to the painting that was actually very appealing. She was proud to hang it in her living room.

"After she hung it up, she noticed a few dark spots she had missed, and some small areas where the dark pigment still leaked through. She managed to scrape away a few of the dark flecks with her fingernail and touched up some of the discolored spots. But she decided it would be more trouble than it was worth to try to make it perfect. She had other things she wanted to do with her time and energy. She now wanted just to enjoy this painting and share its beauty and strength with the people she loved and who loved her."

Helen is now a clinical social worker, engaged in working with families of disturbed children.

For Helen, with respect and affection.

9

The Fallen Tree

A woman in her middle thirties had worked very hard to transcend the effects of a rather harsh and deprived childhood and was rapidly becoming a recognized musician with a promising career.

While visiting her parents in another state, she was injured in a plane crash in which several people were killed. She recovered completely except for nerve damage to her left hand, which left her unable to play the cello. Her career as a performer was ended.

The damage was not visible, so it was difficult for her friends to take her seriously. Even her former therapist suggested that it was primarily psychological (which is why he is a *former* therapist). Her friends were busy getting on with their careers and had less and less to talk about with her. Lydia looked with envy on these friends, who would easily achieve what had also been her dream.

On one occasion, I told her this story.

"There are many different kinds of trees in a tropical rain forest. Some are tall and slender, with leaves only at the very top. Others have branches and limbs all up and down the trunks. Some of the limbs point up toward the sky, while others point straight out or even downward.

"On some the bark is soft and smooth, while on others it is rough and scratchy. Some have large sturdy leaves, while others have leaves that are small and dainty. The fruits may be large or small, sweet or not so sweet. Each tree has its own characteristics, its own functions, its own ways to interact with its world, its own ways to survive.

"This great diversity invites and supports a great variety of living beings. Birds and butterflies, ferns and orchids, monkeys, and even certain kinds of frogs and snails make their homes in the trees of these forests.

"In one of the rain forests of South America, there was a beautiful Lydiamosa tree. (When I told Lydia this story, she did not consciously get the significance of the tree's name.) These trees grow very slowly as they stretch upward, to take their places among the other tall and stately trees of the forest. They reach toward the warm sun that bathes their leaves with light, and stretch their roots outward to find support and nutrients.

"One Lydiamosa tree was particularly striking. The seed from which she had sprouted had fallen under the edge of a huge rock. So as the tree grew, she had to work her way around this obstacle. There was a scar on one side where she had scraped against the rock as she struggled to establish her place in the forest. But she did grow and became a fine tree.

"As the tree grew more and more, she began to imagine what it would be like to be older and taller.

"She gazed upward at the trees whose leaves formed the canopy of the forest. There were great magnificent birds that nested in their branches: eagles, falcons, ospreys and others. The trees seemed so proud to have these noble creatures living in their branches. The Lydiamosa tree longed for the time when she, too, would have a nest of eagles in her branches.

"One day, there was a terrible storm in the forest. The wind pulled and tugged on the branches, and the raindrops beat against the leaves. One of the old weathered giants of the forest was trying very hard to resist. But when a fierce gust of wind struck him, he could resist no more, and fell.

"As the giant tree fell to the ground, one of his heavy limbs crashed against the young Lydiamosa tree. She tried at first to support the falling giant, but he was too heavy. She then tried to squirm out of his grasp, but she could not. In the end, she was pushed to the ground and pinned under the huge limb.

"Finally the storm was over. The young tree felt sore all over. Many of her twigs and leaves had been blown away. Some of her branches had been scraped off as she fell. Other branches were twisted into ugly, deformed shapes. Some of her strongest limbs had been broken.

"Worst of all, she had fallen flat on the ground. Many of her roots had been pulled out of the ground and broken. They were now dangling helplessly from her base. Even those roots that survived were painfully bent and bruised. The young tree wondered if she would die.

"After a while, the tree realized that many of her roots were still firmly anchored in the earth. They still fed her the nourishment she needed to grow and to be strong. But she was pinned under the fallen giant.

"As time passed, she realized that she could point her new branches upward, and they would grow a few feet. But she knew she would never be able to grow tall. She would never be any taller than the little bushes and shrubs that lined the forest floor. She knew there would be no eagles nesting in her branches.

"The young tree was very sad for a long time. Sometimes she wished she had died in the storm. Sometimes she wished that something would happen to her to take away her unhappy life.

"She looked at the other Lydiamosa trees. They were growing new twigs and leaves to repair the storm damage. They were looking up at the canopy above them, that they would soon join. They were eagerly waiting for the eagles or ospreys that would nest in their branches.

"They didn't seem to notice their sister who had fallen to the ground. They couldn't possibly know how her dreams had been shattered. They seemed indifferent to her suffering.

"One day, the young tree heard a strange noise. It was a song, a soft gentle song. She looked very carefully and finally saw a beautiful little green and yellow bird with a patch of bright red on the very top of his head. Soon another bird appeared, and the two of them sang and sang and sang.

"Then the birds left that place and flew all through the forest, staying very close to the ground. It seemed to the Lydiamosa tree that they were looking for something. Maybe they were looking for a place to build their nest, a place that would be safe from the big birds that nested in the tops of the huge trees.

"The young tree looked at her own branches. She remembered how they had been twisted when she fell. It seemed to her now that those twisted branches would be a wonderful place for songbirds to build their home. The grotesquely shaped branches would protect the little birds from any danger.

"She began to rustle her leaves and shake her branches. Soon the song birds saw her and realized that they had found the perfect place to build their nest.

"The young Lydiamosa tree was so excited that she forgot all about the storm. She forgot that she had been pulled to the ground and would never be able to grow tall. She forgot all about her brothers and sisters and the eagles that would nest in their branches. All she thought about was the two songbirds who were able to find a place of safety because of her injuries.

"As time went by, the young tree found many things to be happy about.

"She was proud of how well she had recovered. She was fascinated by the many different kinds of birds and butterflies that lived in the lower part of the forest. She would never have seen any of them if she had grown tall and stately. She loved the beautiful colors and delicate fragrances of the flowers that grew near the ground. She would have never experienced any of these things if she had kept on growing tall.

"She was especially pleased that she could give the songbirds a home.

"Oh yes, there were times when she was sad. There were times when her trunk was sore from the damage of the storm. There were times when she envied her brothers and sisters. Sometimes when the eagles soared high above the forest and swooped down toward the trees in appreciation, she wished she was one of those who was being appreciated. Sometimes she cried when she realized how different her life might have been.

"Then she would remember the songbirds. They seemed to sense when she was feeling sad and would sing a special song just for her. Or they would fly playfully among her branches, as though to say, "Thank you." Or sometimes they would just sit quietly on a twig to share with her the pleasures of an evening breeze and the fragrance of flower that was filling the world with loveliness.

"Suddenly the young tree understood. The songbirds loved her.

"It didn't matter to them what she might have become. It didn't matter to them what her brothers and sisters were like. It didn't matter to them about the eagles' nests. It didn't matter to them that she wasn't magnificent. All that mattered to them was their relationship with her. She was there for them, she was part of their world, and they belonged together.

"Finally the young tree understood some very important things.

"First, she understood how wonderful it was to be alive and to have a place in the world. It was wonderful to be loved and to be able to love in return.

"If someone loved her, that meant that she was loveable. If she gave love, that meant that she was a loving being. Yes, in the depth of her heart, she knew that she was loveable and loving.

"One day the songbirds would be gone. Trees live a lot longer than birds. There would be no one there to love her and for her to love. Oh yes, there would probably be some other song birds some day. But eventually they, too, would leave. Even so, she would still know about herself. She would know she was a loving and loveable being.

"And that has made all the difference."

For Lydia, with great respect.

Part C

A Basic Presupposition

10 ❖

The Heart and The Mind

> The heart has reasons that reason knows not of.
> — Blaise Pascal

> The things a man knows at fifty that he did not
> know at thirty cannot be expressed in words.
> — Adlai Stevenson

When I lead seminars on psychotherapy, I often start with an exercise. I pass out copies of a piece of music. There are many markings on this page of music: sharps, flats, clef signs, notes and all the rest. I ask the group to take about thirty seconds to study this *in absolute silence*.

I then play a recording of that piece of music. I ask people to listen receptively, to let themselves feel the music. The music I use is the aria, "O Mio Babbino Caro" from Puccini's *Gianni Schicchi,* which is about two minutes long.

I then ask people to get a sense of how these two experiences differ — studying the printed music, and listening to the music. Most people find the study of the printed music rather dry, especially if they were able to study it in absolute silence. But listening to the music — that is something else.

To hear beautiful music touches the feelings and engages the heart. The appeal of listening is very strong. When studying a printed page of music, I will try to hum the tune to myself, to give myself something to listen to.

This exercise is an experiential introduction to the differences between the two levels of the psyche I am referring to as the mind and the heart. These concepts are parallel to the different activities and functions of the two hemispheres of the brain — the left brain and the right brain.

Early research into hemispheric functioning might have exaggerated the differences. But there seems to be agreement that the differences are significant. Rather than try to evaluate the research, I wish to elaborate on these differences as being metaphoric of the concepts of mind and heart.

The left hemisphere of the brain tends to process things sequentially. It makes comparisons between one thing and another, or between something and a standard or ideal. It builds its realities one piece at a time, discriminating between options. It processes things in terms of hierarchies and is interested in questions of ethics, power, authority and obedience. It has an intentional, assertive orientation. The left brain is more masculine as we understand masculinity in our culture.

The right brain functions in a very different way. Instead of processing things sequentially, it grasps things in their entirety, embracing the gestalt. It is the world of spatial awareness, visualization, music, art, drama, feelings, intuition, and spirituality. Its mode is more passive, receptive. Instead of taking charge, it accepts.

The right brain is the world of mysticism, aesthetics, vision. It is not easy to talk directly about right brain phenomena because language is a left-brain activity. The right brain generates scientific and mathematical creativity rather than experimentation and computation.

The style of the right brain is more feminine as we understand femininity in our culture. Perhaps most important for the purposes of this study, the right brain seems to be the primary seat of one's world view and is thus the center of change and growth.

The left brain controls the right side of the body, and vice versa. This is called contra-laterality. If one has suffered injury to the left brain, one may be paralyzed on the right side of the body, and vice versa. The way I remember which half of the brain does what is that the right side of the body is thought of as masculine ("the right hand of power and authority") and is controlled by the left brain.

Since most of us are right-handed, the left hemisphere is called the dominant hemisphere. This is true for about 98 percent of the right-handed people and about two-thirds of the left-handed people.

The left side of the body is thought of as feminine (the heart is on the left side of the body) and is thus related to the right brain.

In normal development, both hemispheres of the brain are challenged and nurtured and developed. But inevitably, the style of one hemisphere is encouraged more than the other. In our culture, this is usually the left brain, especially for men. An ideal, of course, is if both hemispheres are richly cultivated and have the ability to communicate easily with each other.

Biologically, there is a bundle of tissues, the corpus callosum, that connects the two halves of the brain and enables them to communicate with each other. In normal life, both hemispheres function in intimate relation with each other, with one hemisphere or the other taking the lead.

Poets have long understood the power of right-brain languages. Take, for instance, the poignant grief expressed by the German poet Friedrich Ruckert over the death of his young daughter:

When your dear mother comes through the door,
and I turn my head toward her,
my glance falls first not on her face,
but on a place lower on the doorframe
where your dear little face would be
if you had come into the room with her, bright-eyed,
as you used to do, my daughter.

When your dear mother comes through the door
in shimmering candlelight,
it is for me still
as though you come into the room with her,
slipping behind her,
as you used to do, my daughter. . . .

(Despite diligent effort, I have been unable to discover the translator of this poem. If you know, please write me so I can give appropriate credit in future editions of this book.)

To express this kind of grief in left-brain language would be impossible.

In another example, Leo Tolstoy writes of a man trying to cope with his impending death.

"Ivan Ilych saw that he was dying, and he was in continual despair.

"In the depth of his heart he knew he was dying, but not only was he not accustomed to the thought, he simply did not and could not grasp it.

"The syllogism he had learnt from Kiezewetter's Logic 'Caius is a man, men are mortal, therefore Caius is mortal,' had always seemed to him correct as applied to Caius, but certainly not as applied to him. That Caius — man in the abstract — was mortal, was perfectly correct, but he was not Caius, not an abstract man, but a creature quite quite separate from all others. He had been little Vanya, with a mamma and a papa, with Mitya and Volodya, with the toys, a coachman and a nurse, afterwards with Katenka and with all the joys, griefs, and delights of childhood, boyhood and youth. What did Caius know of the smell of that striped leather ball Vanya had been so fond of? Had Caius kissed his mother's hand like that, and did the silk of her dress rustle so for Caius? Had he rioted at school like that when the pastry was bad? Had Caius been in love like that? Could Caius preside at a session [of the court] as he did? 'Caius really was mortal, and it was right for him to die; but for me, little Vanya, Ivan Ilych, with all my thoughts and emotions, it's altogether a different matter. It cannot be that I ought to die. That would be too terrible.' "

Tolstoy apparently wrote this story as a gift to his wife after one of their many painful separations.

❖   ❖   ❖   ❖   ❖

Others have expressed these differences in other ways. Johannes Brahms was once asked what he was trying to say in a piece of music. He replied that if he could have said it in words, he would not need to say it in music. Antoine de Saint Exupery said, "To know is not to reason or to prove. It is to accede to vision. But if we are to have vision, we must learn to participate in the object of our vision."

Aristotle said that poetic truth should not be confused with historical, logical or moral truth. George Washington Carver said that to understand a plant that was sick, he would hold it in his hand a long time. He would talk to it and eventually would see the face of God in the plant, telling him what to do to bring healing. Even the physicist Max Planck said that creative science needed ". . . a vivid intuitive imagination for new ideas not generated by deduction, but by artistically creative imagination."

Even things like war memorials can embody right-brain or left-brain qualities. Most war memorials have been masculine. The hero strides forth into battle, assured of the rightness of his cause. People stand before these memorials with a sense of pride.

The Viet Nam Memorial is different. It was designed by a woman and is feminine in nature. It lies below the surface of the ground, like a grave. It symbolizes Mother Earth cradling, embracing the men and women whose names bear witness to their death.

The response to this memorial has been unprecedented. People bring here their grief, not their pride; their hearts, not their minds. People have come just to touch the name of a loved one. They have left letters, flowers, teddy bears, even cookies. A whole warehouse has had to be built to accommodate the many tokens of love and grief that were left as a way to say goodbye. It is unthinkable that anyone would leave a teddy bear at the Marine memorial depicting the raising of the flag on Iwo Jima.

❖   ❖   ❖   ❖   ❖

Here are some examples of the kinds of differences symbolized by left brain and right brain activities, interests and perspectives.

Left Brain	Right Brain
making tables like this	telling stories to illustrate differences
processing things sequentially, one step at a time, such as examining the brush strokes in a painting	grasping things in their entirety, such as viewing an entire painting
evaluations in *Consumers' Reports*	television commercials
philosophy, reason, mind, belief, logic, dogmatism	religion, faith, heart, mysticism
insight, analysis	feelings, intuition
telling what is realistic	telling what is worthwhile
cause and effect	all things inter-related
lecture, persuasion	story, drama, ceremony
linear logic	circular logic
power, authority, control	grace, nurture, participation
rules, ethics, values	aesthetics
language, verbal messages	non-verbal qualifiers: gestures, tone of voice, facial expression
directness, forcefulness	indirectness, gracefulness
hierarchies	equality, involvement
competitiveness	cooperation
Western culture	Eastern culture

secondary process	primary process
crossword puzzles	jigsaw puzzles
middle-class educational approaches, as embodied in education	the "languages" of the poor — this may be one reason why poor kids tend to do poorly in middle-class schools
digital functions, such as words, "I am sad"	analog functions, such as weeping
usually functions within our awareness, or can easily be brought to awareness	usually not in our awareness

A kind of paradox is created if left-brain and right-brain activities are confused. Interpretation of a piece of music would be one example. As Susan Sontag said, "Interpretation is the revenge of the intellect on art." It is like having a discussion with your children about the meaning of a lullaby or a nursery story.

Instructing people (a left-brain activity) to express their feelings (a right-brain activity) is an absurdity that used to be rather common among psychotherapists.

As readers know by now, I am a pastoral counselor as well as a marriage and family therapist. In my pastoral counseling practice I once saw a client who expressed concern because she did not really understand God and religion. I asked her if she ever worked on puzzles or brain teasers. When she finally got the solution, she said to herself, "Oh, I get it."

She had; she often worked the Jumble puzzle in the newspaper.

And had she ever heard a piece of music that sent chills up and down her spine?

She had, and mentioned a favorite selection.

And had she ever seen a drama, such as a movie, that brought tears to her eyes?

She mentioned a recent TV program.

And had she ever seen something visually beautiful, like a nature scene or a painting, that elicited a smile and an, "Oh, how lovely"?

She mentioned some flowers she had seen in a garden.

I said, "The 'Oh, I get it' means that you understood the brain teaser. The chills up and down your spine mean that you understood the music. The tears in your eyes mean that you understood the drama. The 'Oh, how lovely' means that you understood the flower.

And understanding God and religion (and life) is *not* like, 'Oh, I get it!' It is like the chills up and down your spine, or the tears in your eyes, or the 'Oh how lovely.' Understanding God and religion (and life) is a matter of the heart rather than the mind."

Many situations in psychotherapy call for a convincing response. Direct (left-brain) statements often lack persuasiveness — they are the expected thing. I remember a client who had grown up poor, in a very dysfunctional family. She was moderately retarded and had been diagnosed as schizophrenic. After two psychiatric hospitalizations, she was discharged from the Army and was now working as a manual laborer for minimum wage.

I really liked Carrie and respected what she had been able to do with very limited personal resources.

She asked me one day if I liked her. I knew that if I answered her directly, she would not believe me. That would be what I was supposed to say. So I said with a kind of humorous exasperation, "You've got to be kidding! That's the most absurd thing I've ever heard in my entire life!"

She smiled and said, "You like me."

We both laughed heartily. I then told her with a lot of warmth in my voice that I really liked her and valued my time with her.

I remember an incident in my own therapy when I told my therapist that I loved him. Coming from a brash, narcissistic young Turk, this was a very risky thing to say. I still remember how vulnerable I felt, and how sensitive I would have been to anything trite.

Carl replied softly that it would be a long time before he forgot the tone of voice with which I said that. The fact that I still remember this after more than twenty-five years speaks to how affirming that felt to me.

A very depressed client asked me once, in deep despair, if God wanted him to kill himself. While I was desperately trying to think of something to say, I said "Alan, a question spoken like that deserves something more than a trivial answer."

Finally I remembered a passage from the prophet Isaiah that spoke of the Messiah: ". . . A bruised reed he will not break, a smoldering wick he will not quench, but will bring forth justice to the nations." (Isaiah 42:3). I pointed out to Alan that he had certainly been bruised by recent events in his life. The flame of life had often seemed just about gone, but the Messiah was to bind up the bruised reed and gently breathe life into the flickering candle of hope.

❖   ❖   ❖   ❖   ❖

The right brain seems very open to indirect messages. It can receive and act on these messages without one even being aware of what is happening. Milton Erickson had a remarkable gift for embedding therapeutic messages and suggestions in what appeared to be casual conversation. For instance, he devised a way of dictating letters to secretaries who were suffering from headaches. In the text of the letters were words or phrases like "comfort," "relax comfortably," "find peace," "be at rest."

While he was dictating, he would speak these words just a tiny bit more slowly and softly. This indicated inconspicuously that they had a different significance than the rest of what he said, and were to be processed differently. In one famous case study, he sat for some hours with a cancer patient who had been a florist. He talked at length about how a tomato seed rests so comfortably in the ground, finds nourishment and peace, and is so pleased to feel the warmth of the sun.

❖   ❖   ❖   ❖   ❖

A client was struggling with a very low self-esteem, much of which had to do with an ugly scar across her abdomen — the result of emergency surgery for some life-threatening situation. She believed the scar to be so disfiguring she could never consider being naked with anyone, which, of course, precluded marriage.

One day as she was lamenting this disfigurement, I asked if I could see the scar. With considerable reluctance, she pulled up her blouse just far enough to reveal a large scar across her abdomen. I ran my fingers across the scar and told her I hoped the day would come when she would *love* her scar (not "the" scar, but "her" scar). (This was over twenty years ago, before our consciousness that any physical touch could imply sexual abuse. I do not know how I would handle a situation like that today.)

She snapped at me contemptuously, "Why on earth would I want to do that?"

"Because it represents the saving of your life. The scar was the by-product of the surgery that saved your life. It is a dramatic and visible testimony that *your life is worth saving* (spoken softly, with intensity). Every time you look at your scar, you can be reminded that *your life is worth saving, your life is worthwhile.*"

No more was ever said about the scar during the remaining two years of our work together.

A few years later, I got a card from her. She was living in Colorado, happily married and pregnant. She said she had recently been thinking about her therapy. She remembered my touching her scar and hoping she would come to love it. "Love from me for that."

I included this incident in a paper I gave at a psychotherapy conference. A woman whom I had known casually was attending. A mutual friend had told me that this woman, Marcie, had recently had a serious struggle with cancer, resulting in a double mastectomy.

Marcie was having great difficulty in accepting this and did not want anyone to know about it. She could, therefore, not accept support from anyone. She had reluctantly confided in only a very few friends and was feeling very isolated and depressed, especially over the physical disfigurement.

One of the reasons people are reluctant to accept support is that they feel obligated to respond to it. I wondered if the story about the scar might offer support to Marcie in a way that did not call for a response.

When I read my paper to the group, I made eye contact with everyone in the room, including Marcie. When I told about the scar, I repeated the words, "I hope the time will come that you will *love* your scar," looking at Marcie briefly and speaking just a bit more slowly and softly. I then glanced at my paper, made eye contact with a couple of other people, and then glanced at Marcie again when I said, ". . . your life is worthwhile."

After the seminar, Marcie thanked me warmly for my presentation — more warmly than would have been appropriate to our relationship. But she said nothing about the story of the scar. I am certain she did not know what I was doing — that I was offering support in an indirect and non-intrusive manner.

In pre-marital consultation, I point out that the right brain tells what is worthwhile; the left brain tells what is realistic. You need to listen to both of these voices. Usually, people in love are listening only to the right brain; they know only that the relationship is worthwhile. It is wonderful to be in love, to feel all those wonderful feelings. It is wonderful to have your whole world be different, to be cherished by another, to love and to be loved. That is wonderful and is indispensable for a good marriage.

But you need to listen to your left brain also. Is this relationship realistic? Will you be able to pay the bills? Do you share the responsibilities of the relationship equally? Have you found ways to resolve conflict that are acceptable to both of you? Do you come from similar backgrounds?

There is a "honeymoon" to any relationship. If you are lucky, it will last a year or maybe even a bit longer. During this honeymoon, everything is wonderful. You overlook realities that might otherwise be troublesome. You are in your right brain, and the analytic discriminating abilities of the left brain are temporarily de-commissioned.

I encourage people to wait until they have been involved for at least a year or more before even thinking about marriage. It takes that long for the honeymoon to begin to fade and for the romance to begin to find a balance.

The problem is that to tell people this is ineffective because it is logical. It addresses the left brain, which is not very functional during the romantic stage of a relationship. Maybe there ought to be a law that would prohibit people from marrying unless they have been seriously involved for over a year. Behavioral mandates will have more power than logic.

---

[1]Tolstoy, (1960) *The Death of Ivan Ilych and Other Stories,* New York: Signet Books (The New American Library), chapter vi, p. 131 f, translated by Aylmer Maude. Used with permission of Oxford University Press.

Part D ❖

Metaphor and World View

World View

> *My world should be neither too large nor too small,*
> *neither too demanding nor too indifferent.*
> *It should be a world in which I can be*
> *significant but not dominant,*
> *limited but not helpless,*
> *helpful but not overly responsible*
> *loved but not worshipped.*

Some years ago, David Rosenhan, professor of psychology and law at Stanford University, reported on a fascinating experiment: he had eight mentally healthy people (including himself) ask for admission to various mental hospitals. These "pseudopatients" included a pediatrician, a psychiatrist, three psychologists, a housewife, a painter and a graduate student in psychology.

They told the admitting doctor they were hearing voices that sounded something like "Empty," "Hollow" or "Thud." Dr. Rosenhan chose these symptoms because they symbolized the ennui of our culture. Also, he had never heard of anyone else exhibiting these symptoms. Other than disguising their professions and the training that led to them, the pseudopatients were open and honest about every facet of their lives.

The results were astonishing! All eight were admitted, seven with the diagnosis of schizophrenia. They were kept an average of nineteen days before they could convince the staff that they were sane, despite the fact that their "symptoms" disappeared as soon as they were admitted. Having been given the label, "mentally ill," everything they did was interpreted accordingly.

One pseudopatient described himself as having had "a close relationship with his mother but was rather remote from his father during his early childhood. During adolescence and beyond, however, his father became a close friend, while his relationship with his mother cooled. His present relationship with his wife was characteristically close and warm. Apart from occasional angry exchanges, friction was minimal. The children had rarely been spanked."

This history is not only normal but in some ways enviable. But the hospital's case summary stated: "This white thirty-nine-year-old male. . . manifests a long history of considerable ambivalence in close relationships, which begins in early childhood. A warm relationship with his mother cools during his adolescence. A distant relationship to his father is described as becoming very intense. Affective stability is absent. His attempts to control emotionality with his wife and children are punctuated by angry outbursts and, in the case of the children, spankings."

Gregory Bateson did a variation of this experiment back in the 1960s while working at a mental hospital in Palo Alto to study the intricacies of communication. He told their consulting psychiatrist, Don Jackson, that he wanted him to interview a new schizophrenic patient whose presenting delusion was that he was a psychologist. He then told one of the hospital psychologists that he wanted him to interview a new schizophrenic patient whose presenting delusion was that he was a psychiatrist!

These two men then interviewed each other in the presence of the staff. Bateson said that the more sane one of them acted, the more insane the other thought him to be. Finally the psychologist recognized Dr. Jackson's name and the game was up.

All of us approach the world with certain presuppositions. Some are like those generated in the two examples above. They are limited to specific situations and are easily changed. Others are the product of a whole lifetime of living. These tend to be very general and deep-seated. They are not usually in our consciousness, and they tend to perpetuate themselves long after the situations that generated them have changed. These presuppositions taken together comprise our *world view*.

It is impossible not to have presuppositions, not to have a world view. Even animals have world views. I have two cats. When someone knocks on the door, one runs and hides, while the other runs to see who it is. One's world view is that strangers are dangerous. The other's is that strangers are interesting.

When a person's world view is flexible, realistic and enhancing, life goes well. But if one's world view is defective, life will be difficult.

From this perspective, therapy involves helping change one's world view.

World views are formed gradually from the moment of birth, by the untold thousands of experiences a person has in life. For the most part, they are not formed explicitly, by logic and exhortation. They are formed indirectly as a by-product of living, by the story life tells.

World views tend to be self-validating. If my world view allows me to live with some degree of comfort and security, it is never challenged and is thus confirmed. When people treat me like they are "supposed to," that also affirms that my stance in relation to life is satisfactory. Even negative experiences affirm my world view. These are called "self-fulfilling prophecies." If I tell myself that no one will like me, I will most certainly not relate to people with much warmth. And of course they won't like me. The fact that they don't like me then affirms the validity of the original world view.

This is related to Einstein's well known comment: the theory determines the facts. The theory (world view) tells us what to look for in an experiment. It determines what we give attention to and, of course, colors the conclusions we draw. Gregory Bateson expressed it a bit differently. He said that objectivity is impossible. Objectivity simply means studying very carefully something we *choose* to regard as important.

World views are challenged by the unexpected, by experiences that make us feel uneasy. When this happens, we have three basic options: we can dismiss the incident as irrelevant, we can rationalize it, or we change our world views.

Some years ago, two famous television evangelists were involved in sex scandals. Their supporters — those whose world view affirmed that these people lived by the values they advertised — faced some difficult inner decisions. Some, no doubt, simply ignored or minimized the offenses, saying that what is really important is some other aspect of their lives. Others may have denied the reality of their offenses, saying that the charges were made up by people determined to sabotage their ministry. Still others simply changed their world view and realized that these evangelists were not worthy of their trust.

This is not an easy step. When I invest time, energy, feeling and sometimes money in a cause, I get my ego involved in it. To withdraw that investment, to change my world view relative to that cause, I must admit that I was mistaken. That is very difficult for most Americans, especially men!

When I read anthropologists' descriptions of some of the "peculiar" aspects of a foreign culture, I have a rather strange reaction. I begin looking for explanations for those strange behaviors and attitudes. It seldom occurs to me that people of those cultures would find my own attitudes and behaviors just as peculiar to them as theirs are to me. In other words, I take my own world view to be the norm, and anything that differs from that needs some explanation.

One of the attitudes that permeates our culture is the idea that change comes through intimidation. This idea not only influences the ways we raise children and treat criminals but also is present in most marital disputes. "If I can prove I'm right, or if I can make you look bad, then you will change." It is often quite a shock to people to find out that this mentality is not only ineffective, it is not even universal.

In our culture, we tend to be rather casual and informal with our guests. We ask them to make themselves at home and help themselves to the refreshments. But a Japanese guest in an American home would find this attitude to be quite cold and uncaring. It might sound like, "Don't bother me with your needs or wishes. You are on your own; no one will help you to feel welcome." A Japanese host would *bring* drinks and snacks to the guest, while humbly apologizing for their inadequacy.

If I told a client, "Forget your wife, and be loyal to your mother!," we would probably regard that as very strange. Yet in many parts of the world, that is the attitude that prevails. The fact that mother is more important than wife is taken for granted. Any contrary opinion would be looked upon as malicious or insane.

There is a sense in which we create the world in which we live — all world views are to some extent arbitrary. From the many aspects of our experience, we "choose" what will be uniquely ours. We give importance to some things — events, values, characteristics, relationships, possessions — and withhold importance from others. These then become our special world. We create by giving importance.

Four weeks before teaching my daughter Maggie to drive, I had her sit in the front seat with me and comment on everything she saw that was relevant to the driving. A signal ahead had just turned red. A car was waiting on a side street. A pedestrian was standing at a crosswalk. I wanted her to see the world with different eyes, to become aware of the world around her, to give importance to a new category of reality. I felt this was the most important aspect of her learning.

In some cultures, marriages are still arranged by parents. It is nice, of course, if the young people will somehow manage to fall in love with each other spontaneously, without knowing that the parents are wanting them to get together. One technique is for the marriage broker to tell a young man casually, "Have you noticed that so-and-so keeps looking at you?" He will then ask the same question of the young woman.

Somewhat similar situations have been reported with school children. If you tell a new teacher, "Barbara Smith, in your class, is a really outstanding student!," the teacher begins to treat her as an outstanding student, and Barbara's I.Q. will actually rise. I did a similar thing with my grand-children. During Ashley's first months, I watched carefully for any change in his expression while his sisters were looking at him. I would then exclaim excitedly, "Look, he's smiling. He likes you! He likes you!"

Presumably the world of science will forego the wisdom that might be obtained by telling a teacher that a new student is a problem child.

A person's world view can also be influenced by what he or she does not attend to.

During the Cuban missile crisis, President John F. Kennedy sent a strong message to Soviet Premier Nikita Kruschev, warning him that all soviet ships to Cuba would be stopped and searched. Kruschev's reply was bellicose and belligerent. Kennedy and his staff studied this reply for some time. They finally decided to ignore it, to pretend that it did not exist. They withheld reality from it.

The next day, they received a much more conciliatory message from Kruschev, and the crisis abated.

As therapists, we occupy a position of great prestige with our clients. We are in a position to influence significantly their world view, their sense of what is real and what is important. We give reality to the things we ask about and attend to. We minimize the importance of things we do not ask about and do not attend to.

If a client talks about a problem and I look for underlying causes, I imply that those causes are what is important. But if I ask how he or she has dealt with the problem, that implies a very different estimation of his/her abilities and his/her worth. When a client describes a conflict in an important relationship, he or she implicitly defines the conflict as the defining reality of the relationship. If I ask about times when the conflict is dormant, I suggest a different world view.

In doing supervision, I will customarily begin the session by asking students what they have done the past week that they are pleased about. What are their successes? By telling me these, they are affirming their competence. Then when they tell me about problems, it is in the context of their competence. They need not be defensive. We are fine-tuning a system that they have already demonstrated is functioning well.

The same is true with children. If I as a parent focus on what is negative, I give reality to that. But if I focus on their growth and creativity, I enhance their affirmations of those qualities.

❖   ❖   ❖   ❖   ❖

The media are important builders of one's world view. In programming and in advertising we see behaviors and styles of life that imply that certain world views are normal. These take on a kind of mythological quality. They seem to embody something of the essence of ultimate reality.

Family myths can have this same effect. One of the stories in my family that had this mythological significance had to do with my grandfather, for whom I am named. When my mother was a little girl, she wanted to fix a special breakfast for him on Father's Day. But to her horror, she burned the toast terribly.

She presented it to him apologetically, with tears in her eyes. Papa then hugged her and told her, "Why dear, that's just the way I like it." He proceeded to apply butter and jelly and eat it with apparent delight.

This story implied something about the kind of family we were. It was about our sense of what was appropriate and caring — in other words, about our world view.

❖　　❖　　❖　　❖　　❖

In the history of religion, a heresy is where one teaching is taken to the exclusion of other teachings. One teaching is given a kind of ultimate status, and all else is subordinated to that one over-arching concept. Organized religion has tended to deal with heresy by logic and exhortation, appeal to authority, threats, rejection and finally punishment.

For one to live well, one must have a broad repertoire of ways of feeling, living and relating. Ideally, a person knows how to laugh and how to cry, how to stand up for oneself and how to give in. One knows how to ask for help and how to work things out by oneself, how to support and how to criticize.

If one's repertoire is limited, one's life feels cramped. If one's repertoire is severely limited, he or she is given a psychiatric diagnosis. Any one characteristic, carried to an extreme, becomes pathological. In this sense, psychopathology is like heresy. It is a very narrow and constricting world view, a limited range of understandings, a limited repertoire of feelings and behaviors.

For example, to see reality only in the pain in life is to be depressed; to see reality only in that which is cheerful is to live in denial. It is interesting that society has often dealt with the mentally ill the same way that organized religion has dealt with heresy: logic and exhortation, appeal to authority, threats, rejection and finally "punishment" (incarceration).

Here are some unfortunate "heretical" world views:

> Everything is terrible (depression).
> Everything is wonderful (denial).
> Everything is my fault (guilt).
> Nothing is my fault (narcissism).
> If I get in trouble, somebody will rescue me (dependency).
> If I get in trouble, nobody will help me (isolation).
> Everything is terrifying (phobia).
> Everything is secure (naivete).
> I will always fail.
> I will always succeed.
> I will never take a suggestion.
> I will always take all suggestions.
> If I follow rules, the world must reward me.
> Life is not worth living without _____(money, power, sex, a child, good health, etc.)

One thing common to most if not all psychopathology is the loss of a sense of control. One cannot control one's feelings (depression, phobias), one's thoughts (obsessions), one's behaviors (compulsions, addictions), or one's relationships (paranoia). So one aspect of all successful therapy is helping people regain a sense of appropriate control of their lives.

Perhaps the most obvious example of pathology resulting from world view is in marital conflict. Most marital conflicts can be thought of as conflicts of world view (loyalties to the family of origin?). Each insists that his/her world is the only one that any normal person could possibly embrace. The other poor dummy ought to straighten out and acknowledge that. Since each feels that way, the basic struggle is to see whose world view will prevail.

I remember a husband who thought it appropriate to spend every other weekend hunting and fishing with his buddies. His wife maintained that he should spend all his spare time with her and their child. Another wife insisted that it was appropriate for her sometimes to give her husband a suggestion (such as for him to stop yelling at her so much). He actually increased the unwanted behavior to show her that she could not tell him what to do.

Another husband said that his wife should intuitively know when he is depressed and comfort him. She would coldly wait for a specific request before making any move toward him.

If psychopathology is correlated with defective world views, then therapy involves helping clients change those world views. My thesis is that one's world view is primarily associated with the right hemisphere of the brain. To change someone's world view, I must speak the languages of that part of the psyche. That is what this book is all about.

It is important never to attack a client's world view directly. After all, this world view — no matter how dysfunctional — has enabled the person to survive. It has been valid and important, and new understandings must be built on existing understandings. In short, one must begin where the client is now.

Many times in life, that which was once a friend becomes an enemy. But to let go of that enemy, it is important to recognize that it was once a friend. George and Don were buddies all through high school. But in their senior year, George got hooked on drugs. Don tried to help his friend but could not. He finally realized that if he maintained his relationship with George, his own life would suffer. So he had to regard George as a kind of enemy and avoid him. He grieved the loss and got on with his life.

The same is true for many people with addictions. Cigarettes were at one time friends. They were a means of pleasure, of rebelling against parents, of being part of the group, of acting adult. But later one realizes cigarettes are destroying one's health and must regard them as an enemy. It's easier to break this habit if one can acknowledge that the cigarettes were once friends.

All the things we say to clients imply world views. This is especially true of the questions we ask. So in that sense, every question is an intervention.

"How are you going to spend your evenings when you are no longer drinking?"

"How will you and your wife maintain a level of intensity with each other after you are no longer fighting so much?"

"How have you gone about correcting your mistakes?"

"What is different about the times when you are getting along?"

"How do you tell the difference between depression and moodiness?"

"What will you and Dad talk about after you have forgiven him?"

"What are some of the first things that will let you know that inner changes have already begun?"

"Could you think about this time in your life as an opportunity for spiritual growth?"

"Who sees the real you, the healthy part of you, down underneath all the problems?"

"You have come here to make some changes in your relationship. I want to know first what some of the things are that you want to make sure do not change. That is the context in which change takes place."

❖   ❖   ❖   ❖   ❖

For a period of time, it seemed that my nine-year-old granddaughter was getting into snits about almost everything. I asked her once, "How do you go about deciding when something is important enough to get angry about?"

"I don't know."

I persisted with the question. She said that she used to get mad whenever she lost a game, but that she doesn't do that any more.

I replied excitedly, "That's fantastic! How did you go about changing that?"

"I dunno. I just thought it was stupid."

"Well, yeah, but are there some other things you used to get angry about that didn't seem so important later?"

She shrugged her shoulders, and I let it drop, feeling that I had planted some seeds that might well take root some day.

12 ❖

The Utopia Syndrome

> *It is better to light one small candle than to curse the darkness.*

A middle-aged university professor had led an anguished life for as long as he could remember. His psychiatrist diagnosed him as schizophrenic and treated him with medication, but refused to discuss his family of origin and his religion — the two most important things in Fredrick's life.

Fredrick had studied extensively the work of a famous west coast therapist, and concluded that this approach was the one thing that could really help him.

One summer he had the opportunity to spend three months at an institute with this person. He would study and also receive personal therapy. He looked forward to this with enormous hope for himself. At last he would experience the healing touch of the master.

The therapy apparently touched on some very painful areas of my friend's life. But the summer ended before they could reach an adequate healing and resolution. As he started home, Fredrick became so distressed that he was hospitalized briefly. Three days after his return to Miami, he killed himself.

I reflected on how much hope he had invested in his work with this therapist. It was utterly disillusioning for him to find out there was no magic, no ultimate answer to his suffering, no Utopia. He was searching for a kind of perfection, and ultimately the search killed him.

The search for perfection takes many forms. Hoping to find the perfect therapist is one, but there are many others. The basic conviction is that unless at least some aspect of my life is perfect (exceptional, wonderful, and so forth), life is meaningless. I don't know who invented the wonderful term, *The Utopia Syndrome*, but it aptly labels an aspect of one's world view that can be terribly destructive.

Claudine told the mental health clinic staff that for years, she had been praying for God to help her. She wanted the miracle that would resolve the problems in her personal and family life. Finally she realized this was never going to happen. If anything were to change, she would have to do it on her own. So she contacted a therapist and started working on the problems.

Although Claudine felt there had been much less change than she had wished, she recognized that if she had kept spending her time and energy searching for the miracle, *nothing* would have changed.

People sometimes try to *make* themselves do or experience something that can only happen spontaneously. This is a facet of the Utopia Syndrome.

Arnold suffers from insomnia. The harder he tries to get to sleep the more sleep eludes him. It will help if he will give up the Utopia of getting eight hours of sleep a night. Human beings can get by with very little sleep. We have very little control over sleep, but we have a great deal of control over the amount of rest we give ourselves.

So Arnold can simply lie comfortably in his bed for eight hours a night. If he gets bored, he can do something to keep his mind occupied. He might practice the multiplication tables (as I sometimes do), or think of the perfect response to a recent encounter with someone. The amazing thing is that when people do this kind of thing, the subconscious mind does create some sleep.

Many women who desperately wish to become pregnant finally give up and adopt. Often within a year or so, they are astonished to find themselves pregnant. Somehow or another, the obsession to become pregnant was interfering with the body's natural processes. It was only after relaxing that obsession — the search for Utopia — that pregnancy could occur spontaneously.

Sarah complained that her husband was sexually impotent. They had a wonderful relationship otherwise. They were best friends, spent long hours talking together and enjoyed doing things together. But his embarrassment and her frustration over the sexual impotence was more and more of a problem with them.

I asked Sarah if she had any idea how many women would love to change places with her. Most of the marital complaints I hear are from women whose husbands do *not* talk or spend time with them. Sex may be fine, but without a deeply personal relationship it is trivial and often offensive. Besides, there are lots of ways that people can be together physically and even sexually that do not require an erection.

If they could give up the Utopian quest for an erection, they could enjoy their relationship for what it is rather than trash it for what it is not.

❖   ❖   ❖   ❖   ❖

The Utopia Syndrome is often present in the world of feelings. There are feelings about *things,* and there are feelings about *feelings.* If I am sad when a friend dies or angry at an insult, those are feelings about things. They affirm that I am human.

But I may have some Utopian image of myself that says I must never experience any feelings of "weakness." Those feelings then become threatening, and I must get rid of them.

The end result is that I may feel guilty about feeling angry. I may feel ashamed at feeling sad (weak) or angry at feeling anxious. These second-level feelings can be very troublesome.

It is important to know that feelings are just feelings. They don't need to be "commented on" by other feelings. To be depressed, for instance, is simply to be depressed. It is not a disaster. You do not need to say to yourself, "I ought to be above such things. I ought not to be so weak."

The late John Warkentin, a well-known Atlanta psychiatrist, said that on occasion he would feel severely depressed. When that happened, he was determined not to fight the feelings. If he could, he would lie in bed in a fetal position with the covers over his head. He would set a timer for an hour and let the depression sweep over him.

He said an hour was usually sufficient. He could then get on with the responsibilities of the day.

Many people do not react that way. If they are depressed, they get terribly concerned and devote enormous energies to getting over the depression. But people cannot *will* themselves out of a depression or an anxiety attack. If they can simply *accept* these feelings and devote their energies to their overall well being, the depression often loses its power. I may not have control over the depression, but I do have some ability to see that I have an interesting and worthwhile life.

When depression and/or anxiety is chronic, there are very effective psychotherapeutic interventions and medications. But the Utopia Syndrome prohibits some people from seeking psychotherapy or taking medication. They must resolve everything on their own. They must be perfect.

❖   ❖   ❖   ❖   ❖

Two other observations. I used to suffer from severe nasal allergies: hyper-sensitivity to trivial irritants (could there be something symbolic about this???). I would get very angry at my inability to control the nasal itching and sneezing and sometimes would over-medicate myself to the extent of being in bed for a day or two.

I could not (would not?) accept the inconvenience of the itching nose. In my efforts to transcend that imperfection, I created a worse malady. I needed to remind myself of the old saying, "There are many situations in life you cannot make better. You can only refrain from making them worse."

In the world of feelings, if you stay with what is, it will run its course and lead to what's next. If you back off from what is, you have to face it later — often in a less manageable way.

The importance of facing one's feelings was validated in the first serious study of bereavement back in the 1940s. There was a fire in a famous Boston night club, The Coconut

Grove. Many people died, and many others were badly burned, including some whose loved ones were killed in the disaster.

During their hospitalization, many of the burn victims recovered normally. Others with the same medical prognosis were not recovering. The medical team asked Dr. Eric Lindemann for a psychiatric consultation.

Lindemann found that people in both groups had lost loved ones in the fire, but those who recovered from their burns had faced the loss of loved ones and grieved. They talked about their loved ones and the pain of going on without them. They wept. They recovered.

The patients who did not recover were those who did not go through the grieving process. They maintained some kind of denial of the loss. They talked as if their loved ones were still alive. They planned to keep their clothes, their places at the table, and so forth. Somehow, the energy needed for healing was being used up in maintaining a denial system. The patients did not recover from their burns.

Utopia in this case meant not experiencing the anguish of mourning — of remaining superficially cheerful.

The Utopia Syndrome can also cloud many of the decisions we make. Did I choose wisely? Did I get the best possible deal on a new car? Did I choose the right career or profession? Did I choose the right spouse? If I did not, should I not try again?

Jeannette had met a man at work to whom she was immensely attracted. She knew that marriage with him would be better than her existing marriage. But as she thought about that possibility, she realized that after a few years in that marriage, she might meet someone else who promised even more. This could go on forever: always looking for someone better. Or her husband might find someone who would be a better partner. Where does the search for Utopia stop?

Jeannette finally accepted the fact that she and her husband were not ideal partners. But they were the ones who had each other. Only if they stopped looking for perfection could they invest their energy in cultivating the relationship they had.

Harry Truman once said that there were lots of people who could do a better job of being president than he could. But he was the one who had the job, and he was going to do it to the best of his ability.

Many extra-marital affairs may grow from this search for the perfect partner (to whom the person feels so entitled). Affairs are always more fun than marriages, until the world of reality sets in. In an affair, the participants present their images to each other and then react to those images. So an affair is imaginary (image-related). Imaginary relationships are not plagued with the reality of responsibilities, of conflicting priorities and world views. So they are more fun than marriages, which inevitably have a heavy dose of reality in them.

It takes a year or so for the images to begin to crumble and for the participants to realize that they are still the imperfect people they were to begin with. But the search for Utopia has prompted many affairs and led to many dis-illusion-ments (dis-image-ments). It is in the light of this reality that someone once said that all good marriages are dull!

American men are particularly prone to unfortunate images. We have the notion that we cannot be liked, much less loved, unless we are first admired and respected. So we present our accomplishments to the world — the things we think will make other people admire and respect us. What these accomplishments are varies from person to person: physical strength, emotional intimidation, important friends, status symbols, money, intelligence, humor, adventures, religion — the list is endless.

If we are successful, the logic goes, we will then be admired and maybe even loved. If we are not respected, we fear that no one can possibly love us.

There is an old saying about this:

Most of all, I want to be loved.

If I cannot be loved, I at least want to be respected.

If I can't even be respected, I will make myself feared.

After a while, we tend to forget about wanting to be loved, and the demand for respect develops a life of its own. When this happens, men have been known to kill rather than lose face (respect). A Miami newspaper reported an extreme example. A brash young man pulled into a convenience store parking lot. When he opened the door of his car, he put a tiny scratch on the adjacent car. The owner of the other car was irate; the offender would not apologize, the owner would not back down, and the offender was killed.

This demand for respect is even more absurd when it is directed to children, where parents equate obedience with respect.

One of my daughters came in once from a church retreat, saying she had made a commitment to be a more obedient daughter. I told her that she was my daughter, not my dog. I didn't care anything about obedience. Obedience is something I want from an animal, not a child.

I told Cathi I was very pleased with the way she was growing up. She was an involved member of the family, she offered her cooperation cheerfully, she was a pleasure to be around. I didn't care anything about obedience.

Never one to be deterred, she said that nevertheless she wanted to be a more obedient daughter. I told her, "All right. If you really want to be a more obedient daughter, the most obedient thing you can do is to get this notion of obedience out of your mind, and just keep on being the way you are."

When I asked her about this incident some years later, she said she didn't remember it — so I guess I got through to her.

The wish to have obedient children, especially adolescents, is the source of terrible power struggles. Parents inevitably lose. John Warkentin said humorously there is a very sound reason why parents should not get into power struggles with adolescent children: It's a shame for grown-ups to make fools of themselves.

Many of the self-help books on the market seem to promise Utopia. One best-selling title is particularly interesting: *How to Get the Love You Want*. I understand this is an excellent book, but the title seems to promise Utopia. I would rather see a book entitled, *How to Live Well in Spite of the Fact that You will Never Get the Love You Want*. No one is ever loved enough, or wisely enough. No one has ever been loved as much as one deserves. Not only are we human, but all the people around us are also.

A religious variation of the Utopia syndrome says that if one has enough faith, all one's problems will be solved.

From a spiritual perspective, the Utopia Syndrome expresses one's inability to accept humanness, finitude. It's easy to become obsessed with trying to find perfection. One easily becomes stuck in that struggle and may have difficulty getting on with life. Paul Tillich discussed this brilliantly in his remarkable book, *The Courage to Be* (Tillich, P., 1952). He described the inevitable anxiety that is implicit in all living, which he called *existential anxiety*. If people cannot accept that anxiety, but build defenses against it (which can never be satisfactory), they create another kind of anxiety which Tillich called *neurotic anxiety:* the anxiety that grows from the inability to accept one's finiteness, one's humanness. It is this anxiety, to use the language of this book, that accompanies the Utopia Syndrome.

❖　　❖　　❖　　❖　　❖

On one occasion, to bring a gentle ending to a particularly intense session, I told what I thought was a light-hearted story.

"In the early part of this century, the tomb of the Egyptian King Tut Ankhamun was discovered. Among the treasures was a bowl of wheat — food for the journey to the other world.

"This was at a time when people attributed almost magical powers to the ancient Egyptians. So they wondered if this wheat would grow. They gave some of it to a well known agronomist, who carefully planted and watered it. Lo and behold, in a few weeks the wheat actually sprouted!

"This became well known in the scientific community. Never before had wheat been known to maintain its viability for more than seven years. The agronomist's reputation was enhanced, as was esteem for the ancient Egyptians. It even influenced the ways farmers stored wheat. They now kept it dark, cool and dry.

"Years passed and the stories of King Tut's wheat became part of the lore of the ancient Egyptians. It was one of the unfathomable mysteries of ancient wisdom.

"Shortly after the agronomist died, one of his sons published an article about King Tut's wheat. When the wheat was given to his father, he and his brother were teenagers and decided to play a trick on their father. They mixed some contemporary wheat in with King Tut's wheat. They promptly forgot about what they had done until *after* Dad had announced it to the world.

"By that time the whole situation had gone so far that they didn't know how to handle it and so did nothing. So the myth of King Tut's wheat persisted for many years."

Norma listened intently as I told this story and then thought for a long time before asking, "Why did you tell me that story?"

I answered non-committally, "I just thought you might like to hear it."

She was utterly serious in her reply. "I think I have attributed magical powers to you."

Suddenly I understood that for her this was no light-hearted transition to end the session. It was a situation fraught with meaning.

Never one to let a golden opportunity go unutilized, I nodded and said thoughtfully, "I sure did that with my therapist. It was a long time before I realized you could use contemporary wheat to make bread that was really very nourishing and satisfying."

A woman who had never had children married a widower with three teenage daughters. Marian really wanted to be a loving and responsible mother to these children who had suffered such a terrible loss. But the more she tried, the more the kids seemed to resent her. She began to feel angry at their non-responsiveness, then guilty about being angry.

I explained that the kids probably felt that if they let her mother them, they were being disloyal to their dead mother. It would probably take a long time for them to realize that their mother would approve of their accepting love from another woman.

Marian began to recognize that her anger and guilt told her that she was just an ordinary human being, like all the rest of us. As she was able to accept her own humanness, she would be able to accept imperfections in her stepchildren — an indispensable quality for a stepparent.

Three years later, things were a bit calmer. But Marian's efforts to parent her stepchildren were still not fully appreciated. As Mother's Day approached, she very much wanted some recognition. She even wondered about suggesting to their father that he set it up for them to take her to lunch.

"Why not take *them* to lunch?" I proposed. "They've given you a new experience that you've never had before —

the experience of being a kind of mother. Tell them you're grateful for that opportunity."

Marian really liked this idea. She would give each of them a card telling some of the things she appreciated about them. In this way, she would be doing her own affirming, rather than giving that power to kids — who were likely to withhold it.

Utopia for Marian was for someone else to bestow a blessing on her. She so hungered for it that her efforts to get it were beginning to interfere with her living. When she took her own initiative — giving up her Utopian dream — the result was more realistic and the payoff more tangible.

The main thing I do to help people accept their humanness is to tell stories (metaphors). To challenge people's obsession with Utopia, I have often told about the people mentioned in this chapter. To help people accept their humanness, I often tell stories about myself and my difficulties in living. When I tell these with a gentle humor or a calm acceptance, I suggest that the client can also be comfortable with imperfection.

13

The Fall
An Allegory on the Search for Perfection

> *The Lord God sent forth the Man from*
> *the Garden of Eden . . .*
> — Genesis 3:23

The story is told of a young psychologist whose consuming passion was mystical concentration. In the course of his training, he had witnessed many sessions of mystical concentration and had seen many marvelous things accomplished.

It occurred to him that this unique experience had an application far beyond the research and psychotherapy to which responsible practitioners limited themselves. Mystical concentration seemed to him as a key which could unlock a whole new dimension of life. It could enable him to experience areas of life that would otherwise be impenetrably closed.

He turned first to some of his friends who knew this ancient art, to lead him into the depths of concentration. He thus became familiar with the experience and its potentials. But his friends were responsible people and would not lead their friend into abnormal states. In fact, they soon realized the obsession he had about mystical concentration and refused altogether to work with him.

He then turned to self-concentration. His own previous experiences provided a background, and he was soon able to accomplish deep states of concentration. He set aside a small room in which to perform the ritual: mirrors on two opposite walls, heavy drapes on the other two, with candles for light and burning incense for atmosphere.

The two mirrors facing each other provided multiple images of himself and magnified his self-consciousness to the point that it ceased to matter. He was soon leading himself into profound depths of mystical concentration along predetermined lines.

There was one possibility that normal mystical concentration had never before explored. Would it be possible to induce a subject to die? He needed to know if this ultimate power was possible.

He contacted the warden at the state prison and was given permission to conduct an experiment with a prisoner on death row. The prisoner's consent was granted when it was explained that this would not only advance the cause of science, it would also give him a sense of dignity relative to his death. He would, in a sense, be in charge of his death. It would not just be something done to him by the "system."

The execution was eight weeks away, a Tuesday morning at ten o'clock. The agreement was that the final concentration would be that morning. If by ten o'clock it had failed to induce death, the electrocution would proceed as scheduled.

The psychologist planned to work with this prisoner once a day for the entire eight weeks, gradually inducing deeper and deeper states of concentration. On the final day he would simply cause the man's heart to stop.

As the weeks went by, things looked very hopeful. The prisoner was a good subject and was soon being influenced at the level of his autonomic functioning.

But in the process of this work, the young psychologist came to like the man and felt the death penalty to be extremely severe for his crime. He could not in good conscience be his executioner and told him so.

But the prisoner repeated to him the very arguments that had been used earlier, about dying with dignity. Finally the psychologist consented. On the day of the execution, the psychologist said a tearful goodbye to his friend and led him into a deep state of concentration. In a short time the man was dead.

This experiment had produced far more than anyone could have anticipated. Not only was the fact established that mystical concentration could induce death, but a whole new dimension of life had been opened to the young psychologist —– the power over life. An exhilarating thing in its magnificence, it seized him with an overwhelming anxiety and guilt. He had not used violence or brute strength, but only the force of his own personality. He had spoken, and a man had *died*.

This power, this "divinity," was awesome, and he felt a terrible guilt. The guilt rested not so much in what he had done, but in the mere fact that he possessed this power. But the very presence of the guilt augmented the strange exhilaration he felt in his possession of power. It added a depth and mystery that he cherished. Mystical Concentration indeed had opened new vistas of life-experience.

In the succeeding months, he limited his experiments to self-induced experiences. In various ways he altered his own person, so that clothed in different identities he could embrace the full gamut of human experiences.

For one period of several months, he concentrated on making himself become an athlete, to feel the joy of physical self-expression. For another several months, he concentrated on changing his body into that of a woman, that he might know a woman's experience of sex. In both of these strange adventures he was successful. He felt that he had unleashed tremendous powers within himself. He was drinking deeply from the cup of life's joys.

After resuming his original physical and sexual identity, he next wanted to explore some more abstract areas of human existence.

He first went to a meeting of Mensa, that self-conscious gathering of geniuses. He associated with these people for a while and then withdrew to his "Holy of Holies," the concentration chamber. He quickly transformed himself into a genius.

This was a good experience for him. He loved the unaccustomed ease of grasping difficult concepts, of creating brilliant approaches to complex problems, of feeling in total control of his mind. He had determined to experience all that life had to offer, and this was a magnificent step in that quest. But it was not really him, so he resumed his own identity and next set out to explore a more primitive kind of human existence.

He went to a nearby mental hospital and spent a week in close association with a mentally retarded patient. He came to know something of what life was like for this person.

He then returned to his concentration chamber and proceeded through mystical concentration to transform himself into the likeness of this retarded person.

Indeed this was a new experience and for him, a good one. Gone was the nervous apprehension about tomorrow; gone was the frantic racing of his thoughts pursuing some elusive goal; gone was his obsessive drive to excel. He felt himself to be as a child again, to live, to feel, to play, to think as does a child. Another dimension of life had been opened to him, and he embraced it gladly.

But when he was ready to resume his own identity, he found to his horror that his experiment had been too successful, the transformation too complete. He could not remember how to change himself back into himself!

The memory he had of himself was clear, although it seemed somewhat unreal. He recalled his achievements, his experiences of life, his potentials, but how to recapture them? He could not remember. He called on his friends for help, but their efforts were equally futile. The door leading back to himself was locked, and he could not find the key.

H. Close. Originally published in *Voices: The Art and Science of Psychotherapy,* Summer, 1966. Used with permission of the publisher.

A year or so after I wrote this story, I suddenly understood it. It was a story about the search for perfection. In his obsession to experience everything, the young man lost the very self that was the seat of all experiencing. This is perhaps parallel to the story of Adam in the Garden of Eden. He wanted to know (experience) everything — something that was forbidden — and lost something essential in the process.

14

A Young Man and a Mermaid
An Allegory on Limitations

> *. . . to enjoy you for what you are,*
> *and to forgive you for what you are not.*
> — from a contemporary wedding service

T here was once a young man who loved the ocean. As often as he could, he would go to the seashore to rekindle his love.

If it were winter, he would walk along the shore picking up shells, sponges and seaweed that were cast up on the shore.

If it were summer, he would swim. He loved to play in the surf, or to dive into an oncoming wave and feel its force, or to lie calmly in the water to be lifted by a wave and carried along on its crest.

He loved all the moods of the sea: her serenity, her playfulness, her power. He particularly liked the rocky shores, where the waves would expend themselves in an endless symphony of music and a thousand varieties of spray and flow and movement. Then at night he would sit for long hours on the sand and listen to her. The rhythmic pounding of the surf was like a heartbeat, full of life. The smell of the sea was a beautifully sensuous thing to him, a constant reminder that she was the womb from which all life had come.

In the winter he was usually alone by the sea, and he liked this. It annoyed him that other people seemed oblivious to the immense mystery that the sea represented. They could come and go and play and exploit, but without ever experiencing the sense of awe that he did. Most of the other people showed no signs of love. So in the summer, when the beaches were full, he sought the secluded places, where he could experience the sea with the reverence she deserved.

Most of all, he loved to snorkel and dive. He would dive when he felt assertive and energetic. To go right down the bottom and be in the midst of the coral or kelp or fish, or to swim along the vertical walls of an undersea cliff gave him a sense of presence and participation.

He would snorkel when he felt in a more quiet and receptive mood. He generally chose relatively shallow water where he could observe the graceful dance of the myriads of beautifully colored fish close at hand. If he wished, he could easily dive down and pick up something from the bottom.

One day he happened upon a very small island off the Florida Keys. He came to this area often because the water there was clear and warm, and was like summer almost all the year 'round. This small island was hardly as large as a football field. It had a sandy beach on one side, with a few palm trees and sea pines in the middle and a rocky shore on the other side.

Although it was located on the charts, very few people came there because it was so small. There were larger and more luxurious islands nearby that offered the average picnicker a much better locale.

The young man — David was his name — found this island very much to his liking. He would swim out over the rocks and quickly come to large areas of sea life that had not been plundered: sea whips, sponges, flowers, anemones and a thousand other forms of life and beauty and mystery. He would lie quietly in the water and look with fascination.

One day as he was in the water, he sensed a presence of some kind with him. He turned quickly to look and saw the tail of a large fish disappear behind a large coral mound. Slowly and quietly he swam to the area and looked all around. But whatever it was had slipped away. The next day, the same thing happened. He sensed this presence of another being but saw only a blur when he turned to face it.

When it happened again the third day, he realized that this was not accidental. Whatever he had sensed as a presence was there deliberately and was there for him. So this time he did not turn to look. He remained motionless in the water for several minutes. He felt the presence moving closer to him. Finally he saw a shadow on the rocks just a few feet to his left. It looked quite large, perhaps close to his own size, but he felt no uneasiness, only excitement.

Very slowly he extended his left hand and then remained motionless. He felt the presence to be very close to him. Finally he could restrain his curiosity no further and turned slowly to look. This time he caught a glimpse of the creature as it darted away. It was a mermaid! Somehow, the impossibility of such a creature existing did not bother him. He had felt her presence; he had seen her; and it all felt perfectly natural.

As the days passed, they became friends. He would swim out to the coral area in the morning and wait patiently. Soon she would appear. At first their meetings were cautious. They were both very reserved, extremely careful to do nothing that might be frightening to the other.

Then they became bolder. Being the better swimmer, she would swoop under him in the water and look at him playfully, as though inviting him to chase her. And he did, joyfully. Of course she always eluded him, but she always came back to entice him again. Each time she swam a little slower.

Once as she was darting through the water, she suddenly swerved back to avoid a man-o'-war, and his hand touched hers. He was tempted to hold her but did not. She was tempted to draw back but did not. Though the touch lasted but an instant, it was free, full of life and excitement.

That night as he lay on the beach and listened to the breeze humming through the pines, he thought he heard the sound of singing from the distance.

It was several days later that their hands met again. This time it was deliberate, and their fingers interlocked lovingly. Hand in hand, they swam for a long time, until finally they ended up at the edge of the beach. There was no surf, and they sat in the shallow water and looked at each other. It was the first time they had seen each other clearly at the same time.

When he was in the water, he wore a face mask in order to see. Of course she could not really see him when his face was obscured by the mask. If he was in the water without the mask, she could see him clearly enough, but everything was fuzzy to him. She seemed to be able to see equally well either in or out of the water.

But now they were out of the water — partially at least — and saw each other clearly. The words came to him slowly and softly. "You are beautiful." He knew that she would not understand their meaning, but he hoped she would understand the tone of his voice. To his astonishment she smiled coquettishly and replied, "I know."

So they fell in love with each other. There were only a few days left for him to be there, and they spent every possible moment together. He even tried sleeping in the shallow water wearing his mask and snorkel, so he could be near her. But that didn't work. She tried sleeping next to him on the beach, but her body needed to be kept moist. With sadness he carried her back to the water. They realized that each of them was somewhat out of place in the other's world, and they had to adjust themselves to that reality.

They spent almost all of the last few days in the water. It was her world, and she wanted to share it with him as fully as she could. She knew where the most beautiful coral formations were and took him to caves and ledges and sea forests. She was at home with the creatures of the sea. They swam and played among the fish and dolphin and even an occasional octopus or whale. If sharks were around, she knew how to protect him, so they were in no danger.

But this was not his world, and he was always somewhat awkward in it. Like a dolphin, she could inhale a lungful of air and hold her breath for a long time to dive down into the water and play. He needed air tanks and had to be very careful about ascending or descending too quickly. But he loved her world. He loved it for its novelty and excitement and beauty. Most of all, he loved it because it was her world and she was sharing it with him.

In the evenings they would lie together or play together in the shallow water of the beach. This was the point at which their worlds met and they were most with each other at these times. Their love grew, and they wanted to be together always.

But the time came for him to leave, for the demands of his world called him. They parted tearfully and looked forward to the time when they could be together again. During the next few months he thought of all the things he could share with her about his world. When he returned to the island, it was winter, and the water was too cold for him to enjoy.

So this time he took her into his world. He had prepared a wheelchair with special provisions for keeping her body moist. A blanket covered her fish's tail, and she was relatively comfortable even when sitting up. He had adapted his car too, and she loved to ride. Since she was uncomfortable in any kind of heat, he dressed warmly and kept the air conditioning going.

In this manner he introduced her to his world. Flowers, trees, mountains, valleys, waterfalls — especially the waterfalls — butterflies, animals, everything. He loved his world and was eager to share it with her. She loved it too. She loved it for its novelty and excitement and beauty. Most of all, she loved it because it was his world and he was sharing it with her.

A special love for him was the mountains. To see a beautiful mountain was to want to embrace it. This he did by climbing it — touching it all over with his presence. The mountain then became special to him. He was not just a spectator but had invested something personal in it. He was part of it. He belonged there and took with him something of the mountain's essence when he left. He especially wanted to share this kind of experience with Jan — that was her name — but the whole endeavor was just too difficult.

They set out on a fairly easy trail one day. But after only a couple of miles, the maneuvering of the wheelchair became such an effort that they realized it was futile. This was a deep sadness to him, for the mountains were very important to him. It was as though a part of him, a very deep and intimate part of him, was out there, on the mountain. He had to go there for that part of him to be available to him. If they could not go there together, then this part of him could never be shared with her.

So they compromised; they adjusted to the realities of her awkwardness in his world. There was still a lot they could see from the car, and there were many places with broad paths that would accommodate her wheelchair. So as best as they could, they entered his world together.

After several days of being away from the ocean, she grew fatigued, and their time together had to end. Then too, he had responsibilities that made demands on his time. As they returned to their island, they struggled to find ways that they could be together always.

But this was not to be.

In the long run, they had to settle for a very painful reality. Their worlds touched, overlapped, only in very limited areas. She could take him with her into her world for a while. Together they could touch the very heart of it.

But it was not his world, a world where he could live. They could not linger there to feel together the fullness of its power, to feel oneness between them as they were both enveloped by the mystery of that world. It was he who had to leave, always leaving something unfinished, incomplete, unfulfilled. He could not live in her world.

Nor she in his. It was just the same with her as she struggled to find a place with him. She had to withdraw with the same sense of frustration at the incompleteness.

Their worlds did meet as they lay together or sat together in the shallow water at the edge of the beach. There their joy was full. They embraced blissfully, and nothing else mattered.

But this was not a place where they could live either, this narrow margin of mutuality. Eventually he had to return to his world, she to hers. So they would meet as often as they could, straining to reach beyond the confines of their worlds. They would touch for a brief moment the other's world, rejoice in their common world, and then part.

Finally they came to understand that all of this is just the way life is. Their situation was not unique, for no one enters fully into another's world. No one lingers for long in the presence of another's mystery. There is no way to make permanent the surge of joy that flows through people in the moments of their loving. The area of overlapping of any two worlds is limited. They understood all of this, with sadness, and with this understanding came a sober acceptance of things as they were. They would somehow manage not to chafe at their limitations.

And they would cherish all the more each moment in which their worlds touched.

H. Close. Originally published in *Voices: The Art and Science of Psychotherapy,* Summer 1972. Used with permission of the publisher.
   For Jan, with gratitude.

15

The Potted Tree
An Allegory on Leaving Home

There was once a lovely little tree that lived in an attractive six-sided redwood planter. He was cared for by an elderly couple who lived in a very nice home and showered a great deal of attention on the young tree. He was carefully watered and fed so that he felt neither hunger nor thirst.

He was regularly moved from window to window so he could get the full benefit of the warm sun that bathed his branches with light. He was even turned so that the sun shone equally on all sides, making his growth beautifully symmetrical. He appreciated the loving attention that was given to him and rewarded his owners by becoming a beautiful young tree.

There were times when his owners brought guests into their home and proudly displayed their tree. He always enjoyed these times. The guests would comment on how much care must have gone into his growing. Touching his branches to feel their vigor and strength, they would comment on the color and texture of his leaves and the beautiful symmetry of his branches.

Occasionally one of the guests would be very young and sometimes rough. A young boy, for instance, once pulled off a whole handful of leaves, to crush them in his hand and smell them. This upset the owners. After that, they took great pains to protect their precious tree from young children.

Actually, the boy had not hurt the tree. He was startled to experience this strange and rough treatment and was frightened for a moment. But then he felt exhilarated at his branches being stretched and stripped. He welcomed the challenge of resisting and showing that he could take this kind of treatment.

One day, one of these younger visitors brought with him a unique gift. When no one else was in the room, the boy slipped quickly outside. In a moment he reappeared, holding a strange and beautiful creature in his hand. About two inches long, she was sparkling gold with lovely soft fur.

She moved by arching her back as though in defiance of some enemy and then relaxing peacefully as though finishing the performance of a mysterious ritual. In this way, she slowly crawled from the boy's hand to an outstretched leaf on a lower branch. The feel of her soft body and her fur tickled the tree as she crawled along. If he had known how to laugh, he would surely have done so.

From there, she crawled to the trunk, then up and out to the very topmost leaf and began to nibble. This frightened the little tree for just a moment, for he wondered if he was going to be eaten up. But this was ridiculous. This tiny princess was but a fraction of one leaf. She could not possibly take from him more than he could easily replenish.

His fear quickly gave way to pride. He had at last found someone who actually needed him, and he was glad. When she had finished nibbling on that spot, she moved on to another leaf. In moving, she caressed him with her body and her soft fur, as though in grateful appreciation. He felt loved.

The next day, his owners noticed with horror the tiny holes in his leaf. They carefully searched him until they found his companion, whom they promptly removed and carried outside. They then searched him thoroughly for eggs or larvae or other intruders. They seemed greatly relieved to find none.

But the little tree was sad. Not only had the most exciting relationship of his life come to an abrupt end, but he knew there would never again be another. He knew his owners would keep careful vigil over him. If he had known how to cry, he would surely have done so.

One day a long time afterward, as the tree was being moved from one window to another, he happened to glance out into the yard. He was startled to see there another being very much like himself — another tree! He had never really thought that he was the only one of his kind in the universe. But then again, neither had he thought that there would be others like him. That kind of thought had just never occurred to him.

But now he began to think about it, and this awakened a long-forgotten memory. Yes, there were others like him, but the ones he could remember were very small — as he had been himself at that time.

It had been a warm place. He had struggled hard to push his first sprouts from the seed husk and on through the soft dirt that surrounded him. When he had first looked around, he saw many other young sprouts just like himself. These were his brothers and sisters, and for a while they all grew together. But then there came a day when the family was broken up. Each young tree was transplanted into his own private box and sent off to faraway places.

There was much commotion going on with all these changes and the pride of having his own place. The little tree quickly forgot about the others and the sadness of being separated. But now, as he caught sight of another tree, he thought of his family and remembered how good it felt to be with them. He wondered where they were now and if they had forgotten him like he had almost forgotten them. He stretched again to see if he could see the tree in the yard.

As he looked this time, he saw not just the one tree that had caught his attention at first, but a veritable *forest* of trees in the distance. They were different sizes and shapes and colors, rocking to and fro with the wind. He was overwhelmed with joy and stood there transfixed as he gazed at them with admiration and wonder.

As the days passed, the little tree grew very familiar with the world outside his window. He was particularly attracted to two tall, majestic oaks that stood near the edge of the forest. They, too, were well-rounded and symmetrical as he was, and they stood facing each other in a kind of eternal communion. It seemed that sometimes they played and laughed with each other, as the wind tossed them back and forth. At other times, they stood straight and solemn in a quiet dignity.

He noticed the many birds that flew among their branches or sat there to fill the air with their songs. He thought that if the birds were permitted, surely caterpillars would also be welcome, and he envied those trees.

He noticed also that there were many smaller trees beneath these giants. They seemed to be like them and to be striving to grow tall and stately like their parents. Yes, like their *parents*. He suddenly realized that he had never seen *his* parents — or even considered that he had parents. Surely he must have, but what were they like? Were they like the two stately oaks outside his window?

He looked again, and as far as he could tell, he looked very much like the little trees out there! Maybe those tall trees were his parents too, only he had been taken away before he knew them. Maybe he, too, could grow tall and stately, with golden caterpillars free to caress his branches, and birds to nest there and fill the world with singing.

Slowly a yearning was created within him to be like the tall oaks outside his window. No, that's not the way to say it. The yearning was *awakened,* not created. He realized that this yearning to be rooted in the earth had been within him from the very beginning, but it had been dormant, unrecognized. And now it was being awakened.

It was about this time that he looked into the corners of the yard to see what else was in the outside world. To his surprise, he saw a small cluster of shrubs that also looked very much like him. They, too, had smaller shrubs beneath them that were growing up to be like their parents.

These shrubs were *not* tall and stately. They were not even attractive. No birds sang in their branches, and perhaps even the caterpillars avoided them. The shrubs seemed very insignificant compared to the mighty oaks, and the little tree felt sorry for them. He certainly wouldn't want to be like them.

But maybe he *was* like them. After all, he had no way of knowing that the oaks were his parents. As far as he could tell, he looked as much like the one as like the other. From his window, he could not tell them apart except for their size and dignity. What if he were not an oak, but only a little shrub that was being given very special treatment by loving owners? The little tree felt sad and anxious as he considered this possibility.

During the next several months, the little tree dedicated himself to the task of learning everything he could learn about the oaks, the shrubs and himself. He observed, for instance, that the big trees had very large roots that seemed to reach out a long way from the trunk. The little shrubs seemed to have small roots like his own. So he concluded that to grow big like the oaks, he would have to be planted in the ground where his roots could spread. As long as he lived in his planter, he would never grow tall.

He also noticed that not all the trees were as nicely shaped as the two oaks. Trees in the forest seemed to crowd one another and cause each other to grow off-balance into shapes that were weird and bizarre. The little tree thought that he would not like that — he would not like to be that much influenced by the other trees.

One day, he noticed some men bringing to the yard several small trees not too different from himself. They dug holes in the ground, took the trees out of the pots, and planted them in the ground! This opened a whole new world of possibilities. It meant that he, too, could take his place in the outside world, to spread his roots and grow tall and stately — if indeed he were an oak and not just a shrub.

He watched the transplanted trees very carefully. For a long time, they did not grow at all. In fact, two of them shriveled up and finally died. The others, however, began to show signs of growth as they took their places firmly and proudly in the outside world. The little tree realized from this that he, too, could be transplanted, but if he were, he, too, faced the risk of dying.

When the summer was over, a strange transformation took place with the trees outside. Their leaves changed in color from a deep healthy green to colorful and fiery reds and yellows! They were beautiful, and the little tree wondered at this phenomenon.

But soon the leaves began to wither, giving up their brilliance and their life, becoming a dull brown before finally being blown away by the wind. This disturbed the little tree. He thought all of the trees of the forest had died like the transplanted trees, and he alone had survived. His distress was magnified when an ice storm broke two of the proudest limbs of the oaks he had envisioned as his parents.

His distress lasted all winter. He had almost abandoned hope for his kin outside, when the miracle of spring arrived and he witnessed the rebirth of nature. The trees became alive again, with blossoms, buds and then the full beauty of new foliage. From deep within his being, the little tree understood.

This completed his study of the world, and now he devoted his energies to integrating this new wisdom. He pictured himself as a stately oak, dominating the landscape with his magnificence, yet hosting the song birds and the humble caterpillars. He pictured himself enduring the fall and winter, to blossom forth again at the miracle of springtime. He found great delight in these fantasies.

But one day his fantasies were rudely interrupted. He happened to glance out of the window at the two oaks he lovingly thought of as his parents. Some men appeared, with string and hammers and strange three-legged instruments. They walked all over the yard, driving stakes, tying strings to this and to that, so that their strings finally formed a square that included the tallest oak. The little tree felt uneasy about all this — and with good reason.

The next day a huge bulldozer appeared and casually began pushing huge piles of dirt here and there. Just as casually and nonchalantly, it rolled up to the tall oak, placed its blade against the trunk, groaned with effort as it pushed, and prevailed. The next day, the fallen giant was cut into firewood.

The little tree was stunned with horror, and there was no way to express it. He kept saying to himself again and again, "How could something like this happen? How could it happen?" But there was no answer. If only the giant oak had lived in a planter, he could have been moved. But he was rooted to one spot and so died.

About this time, another change was taking place. It was springtime, and from deep within his being, a surge of growth was preparing to take place. New branches wanted to grow, new roots wanted to push out. But the roots had no place to go. They were already pushing against the sides of the planter. If they pushed harder, they would break it. The little tree knew that he had the strength within him to do this. He could exert himself, go with this new urge to grow, and a new housing would have to be found for him.

He knew in his heart that his owners genuinely cared for him. If he outgrew this planter, they would recognize his wish and would transplant him to a favored place in the yard.

On the other hand, he knew that he could suppress this urge to grow; he could withhold himself. No new branches would appear; no roots would push out, demanding more room. But he knew that if he suppressed the urge to grow this time, it would never come back. He could continue his delightful existence in an ideal world, but he could never again summon the energy to expand. It was up to him, and a decision had to be made. He could go with the urge, or he could suppress it.

He tried to consider everything. The outside world offered him songbirds and caterpillars, but it demanded that he commit himself to one spot. If he survived the transplanting, this one spot confronted him with the risk of wind and ice and bulldozers.

The inside world was a consistent world, free from the distorting influences of other trees, free from the agonies of seasonal change, free from risk. He was mobile, beautiful, appreciated. In this protected world, it mattered not whether he was really a shrub or an oak. He was free to imagine that if he had been transplanted, he would have grown into a tall and beautiful oak.

On the other hand, if he *were* transplanted and grew only into a small shrub, he would have been robbed of these exciting fantasies; to risk the outside world would take away his fantasies and leave him only with uncertain realities.

He was face to face with the urging within him. He *had* to choose — to support it or to suppress it. But he was not ready to choose, and the images tumbled through his mind, confused, garbled. Songbirds and bulldozers and other trees and caterpillars and shrubs and seasons and risk and no more loving hands to feed him and care for him. Nothing fell into place. But the urging within him was insistent, demanding that he choose.

And so, blindly groping, he chose.

For Dustin. I have given this story to a few clients who were terribly ambivalent about leaving home. It seemed to enhance our rapport, as they realized that I really understood what they were struggling with.

Metaphor in Clinical Applications

16

Utilization

What is a weed?
A plant whose virtues have not been discovered.
— Emerson

The concept of utilization in psychotherapy is identified primarily with the work of Dr. Milton Erickson. More than any other therapist, he taught us to appreciate *everything* the client brings. Perhaps his own struggles with a terribly crippling case of polio as a teenager impressed on him the value of regarding *everything* as a potential asset.

Whatever the client brings should be regarded as valuable. Physical defects, personality quirks, vocation, hobbies and symptoms can be used in the service of change and growth. All negatives have within them the capacity to become strengths.

In many ways, this is a simple concept, but it has enormous implications. It is like remodeling a home. Instead of tearing down the old home and building another, the remodeler looks for value in everything about the existing structure. Many imperfections can be altered slightly so that they become quaint. Some things can be highlighted, while others can be de-emphasized. But everything is used.

When I utilize an undesirable characteristic, I am in a sense forgiving people for being the way they are. I add a bit to their self-esteem by seeing value in what they are. I affirm something in which they have invested themselves, however unwisely.

❖   ❖   ❖   ❖   ❖

My office is in a church building. I was talking once with a young woman who was painfully aware that her personal resources were quite limited. As we were talking, the church bells struck the hour and started playing a hymn. Since she was musically oriented, I began to talk about how few notes there are on the musical scale. But these few notes can be put together in sequences and harmonies and rhythms to create an incredible variety of beautiful music.

As I talked about this, there were tears in her eyes. At the end of the hour, she thanked me for the session with a special warmth.

Freeman Dyson, a Nobel laureate in physics, tells of a somewhat similar incident about his father, who was a tutor in music at Marlborough. Dyson asked a new student, Beverley Nichols, to play something for him.

As Nichols sat at the piano, he heard a bell tolling in the distance. He began to improvise, following the tempo of the bell and allowing the melody to dictate itself.

His tutor suddenly turned and asked what that was he was playing.

" 'Nothing, sir. I was making it up.'

"He seemed about to speak. Then he strode over to the piano, ... pushed me aside, sat down and replayed the piece that I had . . . . just invented.

"This was, I think, one of the few supreme moments of my long life. In it I lived more intensely than in any ecstatic climax of passion or of prayer. . . . A great musician had taken this melody of mine that had drifted so fortuitously through the window with the bell, and was developing it with all the resources of his technique and his art. And I knew, and he knew, that it was beautiful."

If events are not noticed and utilized, if they are ignored, then an attitude akin to denial is fostered. Like anything else, this characteristic is sometimes useful, sometimes not. A person with chronic physical pain needs to learn how to ignore things. But more often, denial is a curse. If we recognize and utilize the events that come our way, then we help cultivate an attitude of acceptance.

❖   ❖   ❖   ❖   ❖

I stopped in a craft shop while on vacation in New England. There were no other customers in the shop, so I struck up a conversation with the proprietor. A woman in her middle thirties, she looked like she was having a hard time emotionally.

She responded to my interest in her by saying that the past few years had been very difficult. Her brother had died, and she had just broken up with a man who was very important to her. She was working in the craft shop for the summer to try to get a new sense of direction for her life.

She was seeing a therapist, so it was not appropriate to engage her in therapeutic conversation. Besides, my time was very limited. But I could not not respond. I noticed in the cabinet a helmet shell — a rather remarkable species of mollusk that develops a very thick lip for protection against predators.

I asked to see the shell, and told her that this shell has a very unusual way of growing. The animal feeds for a long while, storing up calcium in its blood. Finally the animal is ready to enlarge its shell to accommodate its own growth. It buries itself in the mud where it is safe and then engages in a remarkable growth experience.

The flesh of the animal dissolves away the thick outer lip of the shell — its defenses — storing up even more calcium in its body in the process. With its protection gone, it is essential that it remain buried in the mud. The animal then uses the calcium from the old lip, plus whatever else it has accumulated, to enlarge the shell and to create a new lip for protection. Only then does it come out of the mud to continue life as usual until the next growth cycle. I told her that I thought she might like to know that this pattern existed in the world of nature.

My friend David provides us with a good example of utilization from his own practice. He saw a client, the daughter of alcoholic parents, who was having a very difficult time with intimate relationships. Shelley longed for someone to love but was terrified when anyone would start to get close. She would panic and either withdraw or attack the person with criticism and rejection. She realized that she did this but was unable to change.

Since Shelley worked in a veterinary clinic (and seemed to feel more comfortable relating to animals than to people), David decided to use her comfort with animals as a kind of model to help her be more gentle and loving with herself. On several occasions, when she would describe some painful event in her life, he would ask something such as, "How would you treat a little kitten that had suffered that kind of thing — perhaps it had been abused and was frightened? Would you be critical of the kitten for being frightened? How patient would you have to be with the kitten? What might you do that would slowly build trust and confidence in this frightened kitten?"

When Shelley castigated herself for the ways she treated someone else, David would ask, "If a kitten were to behave that way, what would you think caused it? What might you do to help the kitten change?"

David told me Shelley greatly appreciated this intervention and did begin to utilize her profession as a model for being more patient and caring with herself. I do not know the long-term results.

I saw a family once for a single session. The new stepfather, who had had no kids of his own, was being something of a tyrant with his preteen stepkids. They were reacting as you might expect. He was captain of a charter fishing boat, accustomed to telling people what to do and having them do it. He could not understand why this approach was not working with the kids.

Near the end of our hour together, I asked him about the different tactics he used to catch different fish. He said that for marlin, you actively troll the waters, going aggressively after the fish. But for snapper, you anchor the boat, let your bait rest on the bottom and wait for the fish to take it.

I told him I thought he was trying to "hook" these kids into a relationship with him as though they were marlin, but perhaps they were more like snapper. Perhaps he needed to put the bait out and patiently wait for them to take it. Maybe when they are irritable and impossible to get along with, he could remind himself that these kids are snapper, not marlin.

His reaction led me to believe that he had heard me and would take me seriously. I am equally sure that he would have abruptly rejected any direct suggestion that he be more patient with the kids.

A client consulted a therapist in order to stop smoking. He was an attorney who had taken off several months from his law practice to help manage a gubernatorial campaign. The therapist asked him to talk about his work in the campaign. The client became animated as he told of working twelve to fourteen hours a day to help accomplish something he really believed in.

He showed a tremendous energy and vitality in talking about the assets of his candidate and the things he stood for. He was equally emphatic about the liabilities of the opponent and what he stood for. He talked about how he marshalled various resources to promote his candidate and to discredit his opponent.

He said that when his candidate won, he felt a strange kind of ambivalence. On the one hand, he was delighted and proud and felt he had made a real contribution to the well-being of the state. But, on the other hand, he felt a kind of letdown. He knew his candidate was not perfect. What if his trust had been misplaced?

The therapist then suggested that he think of his determination to conquer his addiction (not "stop smoking": it is almost always better to phrase things positively rather than negatively) as a campaign. He could direct the same energy and enthusiasm toward this worthwhile campaign as he had toward the gubernatorial race. He could focus on the advantages of his "candidate" and the liabilities of his "opponent" as he worked to install a "government" that truly had the well-being of the system at heart.

The therapist pointed out how elated he had been at the success of his first campaign but also commented on the letdown. No success is ever as satisfying as you anticipate it will be. When he feels a letdown after conquering his addiction, he should simply take this as part of the price a person pays for a successful campaign.

If the gubernatorial campaign had lost, the therapist would have emphasized how disappointed the client felt. It would be a happy contrast when his other campaign (to conquer his addiction) succeeded.

My friend Lettie Mohammed works in a residential halfway house for seriously disturbed patients. One of the patients — a large and intimidating-looking man named Mike — broke one of the rules by meandering through the neighborhood singing loudly. One of the staff reprimanded him sternly and took away some of his privileges.

By the time Lettie arrived in the evening, she found Mike pacing the floor, angrily muttering about what he would like to do to this place.

After finding out what had happened, Lettie reminded him that he had played football in high school. She reminded him that when you are on the defensive line, you have to wait until the ball is snapped before you go charging across. If you jump across the line impulsively, you will get a penalty. Also, when you tackle the runner, you get up, and then you put your hand down to help up the guy you just tackled.

If the referee penalizes you — even if he has made a terrible mistake — you accept the penalty and go on with the game. If you get into a fight with the referee because of his dumb mistake, you get thrown out of the game. It is really important in football to control what you do, even when you would like to do something very different.

Mike seemed a little less agitated as Lettie talked. He sat down in a chair and began squirming, hitting himself on the legs and condemning himself. Lettie asked him if, when he was a little boy and made a tiny mistake (notice the nice reframing), his Daddy would sometimes hit him and call him terrible names. Mike nodded. Lettie then asked if he was doing to himself some of the things his Daddy used to do to him. When he agreed, Lettie said that maybe he could begin to treat himself differently than his Daddy used to.

He then began shaking his arms, as though flinging water off his hands and fingers. Lettie said, "That's right, shake all those bad feelings out, just let them all drip off the ends of your fingers." By this time, Mike was calmer, so Lettie led him through a simple relaxation exercise (counting backwards from twenty in synchronization with his breathing).

Later that evening, Mike told Lettie that if it hadn't been for her, the whole kitchen would have been torn up. Still later, he told her that she had kept him from going back to the hospital.

❖   ❖   ❖   ❖   ❖

I saw a high school senior to help him with his SAT testing. The boy's older brother had scored well on the SATs (1150 or so), but Bert made only about 750 — not enough to get into the college of his choice. He said he knew the material, but if he came to a question he did not understand, his mind just went blank, and he did poorly from that point on.

I knew I could not keep his mind from going blank. What I could do was normalize his reaction, so it did not create panic and discouragement.

I decided to utilize the competitiveness of the two brothers. When he was in a hypnotic state, I told Bert, with much elaboration, that it was not proper for a younger brother to do better than his older brother on any kind of test. In order to make sure that he did not do better than the brother, he should deliberately let his mind go blank on at least one question in each section of the exam.

This somewhat paradoxical approach has sometimes been called "prescribing the symptom." In order to give the client some control over the symptom, the therapist suggests he or she deliberately create it. That idea was probably in the back of my mind. What I was conscious of was wanting to normalize the symptom so it did not create panic.

When Bert took the exam again, he raised his score by some 150 points and was admitted to his university. While it is true that people taking the exam a second time usually raise their score by several percentage points, Bert's 20 percent improvement seems worth reporting.

❖   ❖   ❖   ❖   ❖

A recovering alcoholic was full of guilt over the terrible harm he had done to his family. A previous therapist had tried to work with him about the guilt but was unsuccessful.

I told him he could always trust his subconscious mind to have his best interests at heart, and he should respect that. If his subconscious mind is creating a lingering guilt in him, that may be for a very good purpose. Maybe he is not completely free yet of the capacity to hurt his family. Maybe his guilt is a reminder of his new commitments and his need to keep on growing. I thought he should keep some of the guilt as long as he needed it. When he no longer needed it, it would evaporate. But I thought it would be a mistake to get rid of it prematurely.

A similar approach can be taken with people who get angry and abusive. There will be times when the tremendous energy and determination that are in anger will serve them well. If someone tries to hurt your child, you need all the anger, hate and determination that you can possibly get to protect your child. Don't get rid of abusive qualities; save them to use in a really appropriate situation.

A woman talked about how suspicious she was, to the point that her friends called her paranoid. I pointed out that we live in a violent culture, and her paranoia seemed appropriate to me. When I found out that she drove with the doors to her car unlocked and did not have a burglar alarm in her home, I told her she was not paranoid enough. She needed to mobilize all the paranoia she could, until she had taken appropriate measures for her own safety.

❖   ❖   ❖   ❖   ❖

Joe, a really nice seventy-three-year-old man, consulted me because of a lingering anxiety following a serious illness.

His parents had immigrated here when Joe was a child. His wife died a few years ago, and he had been living since that time with his daughter. He had become very dependent on her, especially during his illness, and suffered extreme anxiety if she left for more than a few minutes at a time.

The first two sessions were with Joe and his daughter, exploring family interaction. The third session was with Joe alone. I reminded him of some of the many things he had learned as a child, such as crawling, standing up, and walking. The memories of the courage and confidence needed to take those steps toward independence were still with him.

The fourth session opened with Joe telling me he felt so much better that this would be our last meeting. About half way through the hour, he told me that his mother had the gift of healing.

He walked over to me and took my arm in his hands. If someone had a broken arm, his mother would take the arm in her hands, manipulate the bones and put on a cast of egg white and plaster. In just a day or so the pain would be totally gone and the arm well on its way to healing.

I regarded this as a comment on the healing he had gotten from me and also as an opportunity for utilization. So toward the end of the session, I went over and sat next to him. I told Joe I wanted to do something, and I would like for him to close his eyes. I took his arm in my two hands as he had done mine and told him that his mother's touch had the power to heal. It could heal a broken bone; it could heal pain. It could heal other things as well.

Joe still had within him the memories of his mother's touch and the power of that touch. And my hands could symbolize his mother's hands and awaken the same memories of healing that his mother's touch could. The same healing can come from a touch that symbolized his mother's.

That touch can heal many things: a broken arm; courage that has been damaged; confidence that has been injured. It can heal anxiety and distress. It can heal injuries to the spirit as well as injuries to the body. And Joe could use those memories of the healing power of his mother's touch that was symbolized by my touch.

I put his arm down and noticed that he was in a deep hypnotic state. I said a few more things about letting those memories stay with him and continue to work for him. When he reoriented himself, he looked at me with tears in his eyes. He said he felt much better and *knew* that everything was going to be all right. He hugged me as he left the office, thanked me warmly, and reaffirmed that everything was going to be all right.

When I was first learning hypnosis, I saw a woman with severe asthma that was dominating her life. She was going to the emergency room an average of three times a week with asthma attacks. She had quit the job she loved to take a job in a doctor's office. The doctor for whom she worked was a very abrasive woman, and Lois was extremely sensitive to insults.

Lois was convinced that hypnosis would help. During our first session I told her (while she was in a hypnotic state) that she had often experienced spontaneous relaxation of tense muscles. Starting at her forehead and working down to her toes, I mentioned every muscle I could think of that was sometimes tense and then relaxed. I told her that she already knew, though perhaps not consciously, how to relax muscles that had become tense. She could transfer this learning to the muscles of her throat when she felt an asthma attack coming on.

On the third or fourth visit, when she came out of the hypnotic state, she told me with some alarm that she couldn't feel anything in her legs. As a beginner in the use of hypnosis, I was horrified at the thought that I had done something wrong and wondered how in the world to remedy it. Then I remembered Dr. Erickson's philosophy of utilizing *everything*.

I told her it was wonderful that she had that numbness in her legs. I would like for her to go back into a hypnotic state and really feel that numbness and its power, and then let the numbness creep up her legs and through her body. Let it come to rest in that place in her psyche where she was sensitive to insults. I thought that would be an excellent way to use that numbness.

She told me the next session that she had been particularly feisty during the week. I took this to mean that she was no longer as intimidated by her boss's insults.

After just a few sessions, the asthma disappeared. Several years later, she told me that sometimes she could feel an attack coming on and would go into a hypnotic state to deal with it. Sometimes she needed an inhalant. But only three times in the next few years did she need to go to the emergency room.

An energetic and vivacious young woman consulted a colleague for therapy following the breakup with her fiance. She came to realize that he was too dependent on her and had actually been abusing her financially and emotionally.

She also realized that this had characterized other past relationships she had had. She wanted to do something about the part of her that attracted inadequate and manipulative men.

One night, she had volunteered along with several others to be a subject for a stage hypnotist at a night club. He had them do some silly things, reoriented them and dismissed them. But Melanie felt that she never came out of the trance. It was like she was in a daze and could not quite be her old self again. Her friends noticed it immediately as did her therapist the next day. Since he did not do hypnosis, he referred her to me.

I listened carefully to her situation and gave lots of attention to matters of rapport and trust. I then asked her to enter again as deeply into hypnosis as she did at the night club. Let herself follow the same path the stage hypnotist had presented.

I then told her that her subconscious mind was always working for her well-being. She could always trust that. The fact that she was still in a daze from the stage hypnosis meant there was something she needed to learn from that experience. Her subconscious mind was using this as a means of getting her attention.

I did not know what kinds of things she needed to learn, what she needed to attend to. But at some level in her psyche, she knew. I thought that maybe one important thing she needed to learn was not to make herself vulnerable to the wrong people. She had done that in the past with men she was involved with; she had done it with the stage hypnotist. Maybe her subconscious mind was screaming at her, "Stop making yourself vulnerable to the wrong people!" I said that maybe she needed to stay in a kind of daze until she really took that seriously.

I then reminded her that she had entered into a deep hypnotic state with me. She could be confident of her ability to enter hypnosis for any *worthwhile* purpose. She could also be confident of her ability to *refrain* from entering hypnosis if the purpose was not worthwhile. Someone else's amusement is *not* a worthwhile purpose.

Two days later her therapist called to say that Melanie was fine and had really appreciated our work together.

A young man came to therapy because he was exposing himself to women. The therapist (Dr. John Warkentin) took this behavior symbolically. He said that many people thought of therapy as an opportunity to "expose" themselves to another person in a way that can be beneficial. He hoped the client would make very good use of his experience in exposing himself.

Another client, a very paranoid man, kept obsessively looking through his closets, fearing what he would find. The therapist suggested he use that energy to look through some of the closets of his memory. He could retrieve whatever was there that could be used in his present life and growth.

A young woman had recently lost almost a hundred pounds and wanted to make sure it stayed off. I discovered she was terrified of spiders. I told her it would be a shame to let a powerful phobia like that go to waste. I suggested that when she got the urge to overeat, she visualize a nice big spider sitting atop the excess food. Or the spider might be in the box of crackers that she knew she should not eat.

I thought that would be an excellent way to make use of the phobia. She agreed and felt that really helped her through some difficult times.

❖   ❖   ❖   ❖   ❖

A woman consulted her pastor because she hated her new baby. She had come from a very complex family background. Her mother, who was white, was a night club singer and away from home a great deal on trips. Her father, who was black, was emotionally unavailable. He finally left the family when she was about five, and she was devastated. Her relationships with men had generally been painful.

She thought of herself as neither black or white. When she filled out forms that asked for her race, she checked all the boxes, or said "all of the above," or wrote in "human."

She was fine with the pregnancy until at birth she saw that the baby was a boy. For some reason that touched a deep hatred. From that moment, she has hated this child. It would have been fine if the baby had been a girl. She said the baby was in no danger from her, but she was very unhappy about him and about her own hatred. She had seen three therapists, none of whom could help her.

The pastor told her that there were lots of distinctions between people in life: boy/girl, rich/poor, tall/short, fat/skinny, smart/dumb, black/white. She had described very beautifully her ability to transcend one of the most important of those distinctions — the racial. She had affirmed the underlying reality of being a human being. She did not think of herself as either black or white, but just as human.

She already knew how to transcend those distinctions, and she could let her racial neutrality be a guide to gender neutrality. She could apply that same wisdom to the sex of her baby, and see this child as simply a human being, a baby, rather than as a boy or a girl.

The pastor told her that for all practical purposes the gender differences do not mean anything until adolescence. If there is a deep-seated need for her to hate a boy, she will have plenty of time to do that during his teenage years. In the meantime, she can just love and enjoy this baby, knowing that it is neither boy nor girl — just baby. (I know this last argument is not accurate scientifically, but it was emotionally relevant for this woman.)

All of us have a vast reservoir of things we have learned that can be utilized symbolically in the service of change and growth. For instance, I often describe the processes by which people learn how to crawl, to stand up, and to walk. There is confidence and courage and satisfaction involved in those achievements. I will then describe some present situations in which these learnings may have symbolic significance: learning how to stand up for oneself, or taking a stand, or taking a step forward.

Some other common learnings are: speaking, reading, writing, riding a bicycle, swimming, driving a car and so forth. I suggest to students that they take a couple of these areas and write out elaborate statements that describe not only the activity but also ways that it is symbolic of some common growth issues.

Phyllis was a clinical social worker in her mid-thirties. She was married with two children and was generally a very happy person. But for as long as she could remember, she had been terrified of birds. When she was a child, her siblings could strike absolute terror in her heart by chasing her with a bird feather.

I first met Phyllis one summer. Her cousin was my client and invited Phyllis to come with her to a session, to explore the use of hypnosis. I talked with her for about ten minutes at the close of the hour, dealing with the bird phobia. At that time, I could not think of anything really pertinent to say about the phobia, but I reminded her (while she was in a hypnotic state) of some of the basic challenges of living that she had met and conquered in her own past. I said that the same courage that enabled her to accomplish those things was still available to her and could be used in other areas of her life.

Several months later my client said that Phyllis was going to visit again and would like to see me alone. This time I had time to prepare. Early that morning I jotted down as many things as I could think of that birds had symbolized. Armed with that, I saw her later that day.

First I asked about the value of the first session. She said it had been quite helpful. She was not yet comfortable with birds, but the terror had abated significantly. She had a down comforter at home, and sometimes the tiny feathers would escape from it during the night. She said she could now pick up these feathers from the floor and discard them. Before our first session that would have been unthinkable.

She again responded quickly and easily to a simple hypnotic induction. I told her that there were many situations in life where things had one significance for a child, but a very different significance for an adult. The significance of something can change with time.

When she was a little girl, she learned that stoves were dangerous. A stove can burn a little girl. She should be very careful around a stove. She learned not to reach her little hands over the top of a stove, because she could be badly burned. Or she could pull over a pot of hot water on herself.

But as she grew older, the significance of a stove changed. She learned that stoves were useful. You can cook on a stove to prepare food, to nurture and strengthen yourself so you can meet the challenges that confront you. And you still have in the depths of your subconscious mind the memories of how you made that change in the significance. It was once something that was frightening; it is now something that is useful and valuable.

Also when you were a little girl, you learned that knives and scissors were dangerous. A little girl could cut herself, hurt herself with knives and scissors. But when you became an adult, you realized that knives and scissors are also useful. They are a means to separate yourself from things you don't want.

I then reminded her that lots of children have been tormented by other children. Some obnoxious little brat may chase a little girl with something in his hand to scare her. Maybe it is a frog or a snake. Maybe it is a bird feather.

It is easy for a little girl to attach her fright and anger to the wrong thing. She may attach her fright and anger to the *thing* rather than toward the obnoxious little brat who is chasing her. As you grow older, you can understand things differently. You can know that negative feelings are appropriately directed at the aggressor, not the thing the aggressor is using.

I then told her that birds had symbolized many different things at different times.

The first robin of spring symbolizes hope. A popular song speaks of the bluebird of happiness. A dove symbolizes peace, even as a hawk symbolizes aggression.

The owl symbolizes wisdom and understanding. The ugly duckling symbolizes how painful it is to be misunderstood and tormented by thoughtless people around you. But finally you find your rightful place in the world where you really belong and where you are appreciated and cherished. The peacock symbolizes flamboyant color. The swan symbolizes grace and beauty.

Even Jesus spoke of the birds of the air as symbolizing God's loving care and protectiveness. The migration patterns of birds symbolize the immense mystery of life that even scientists cannot understand.

I then returned to the first series of comments. I reminded Phyllis that as a little child she had learned that streets and roads were dangerous. They should be feared. But as an adult, you realize that streets are the road to freedom. You have changed the significance of streets for yourself. And you really do know how to change the significance of other things also, from fear and caution into value and enjoyment and freedom.

I did not ask Phyllis for feedback; that might interfere with the healing process. But I felt that seeds had been planted that would be helpful to her.

I wish I had told her to get an identification book on Southern birds. She could learn the names of common birds in her area. To be able to name something gives one a sense of control. It would give her something else to do with her concern about birds.

When she encountered a bird, she could first try to identify it. She might then find herself thinking that she used to have some kind of reaction to birds, but she couldn't remember just what it was. She might be consumed with curiosity about what kind of reaction it was that she was used to have. Then after several seconds she might find the curiosity leaving so she could just enjoy one of nature's really interesting creatures.

A middle-aged psychologist had emigrated from Greece to Atlanta and still spoke with a strong accent. He was lamenting this one day when a colleague pointed out that it could be a significant asset. When a person consults a counselor, he or she is inevitably in a one-down position and may be extremely sensitive about that. The therapist's accent and awkward grasp of English may help neutralize the client's sense of inferiority. It could also be a point of identification. Many clients have had a hard time being understood and have felt isolated — like foreigners in a bewildering world.

Milton Erickson said that when he first went to work at a mental hospital, the superintendent told him he didn't know how Erickson got his limp (it was from a severe case of polio when he was seventeen). He had gotten his own limp in the war. Erickson's limp would be valuable in relating to male patients because it would defuse their competitiveness. And female patients would want to mother him.

A woman had consulted a hypnotherapist for help to stop smoking. Things went fine for a while, but then the therapist started to push. The client felt herself balk at this, came out of the hypnotic state and could not re-enter. After much discussion and effort, the therapist finally said the client was too resistant for hypnosis to be effective, and terminated their work together.

I told her that I thought her resistance was wonderful. She was strongly, adamantly, stubbornly resisting an unwanted intrusion into her life. She would not submit to something that she felt was not in her best interest. This sounded to me like the very thing she most needed to enable her to stop smoking.

She needed to mobilize every bit of that resistance and use it to deal with this other unwanted intrusion — her compulsion to smoke. Her resistance would be very valuable in conquering the temptation to defile her lungs.

She said she was not ready to stop smoking just yet. But with this new perspective, she felt confident that she would eventually succeed.

17 ❖

Metaphor and Reframing

> *Circumstantial evidence is a very tricky thing. . . .*
> *It may seem to point very straight to one thing, but*
> *if you shift your own point of view a little, you may*
> *find it pointing in an equally uncompromising*
> *manner to something entirely different.*
> — Sherlock Holmes
> *The Boscomb Valley Mystery*

A few years after World War II, a woman wrote a book describing her experience as a career Army wife. One incident was particularly instructive. Toward the end of the war, her husband was temporarily assigned to a post near Palm Beach, Florida. One evening they went for a drive along the beach. Both were dressed casually.

Suddenly, a siren sounded as a Military Police jeep pulled them over to the side of the road.

"The MPs alighted and walked over to our jeep.

" 'You've got a government vehicle and a dame in it,' the toughest of the soldiers snapped. 'Let's see your trip ticket.'

"(Wayne) had neither permit nor trip ticket, of course. But he did have his. . . overseas cap on the seat beside him. He popped it on his head quietly, but fast, while the MPs were digging in their jeep for the forms on which they planned to charge Wayne with every violation in the book. They got their forms, turned back to us, and stopped dead in their tracks, openmouthed.

"Four stars!"

Every event takes place in a frame of reference. Its meaning depends as much on the frame of reference as on the event itself. When the frame of reference changes, the event takes on a different meaning and significance. This is called reframing.

The MP approached the couple in the jeep with one frame of reference. He thought these were civilians whom he could bully, and he acted on that understanding. But when he saw the four stars on the field cap, he experienced the sudden, catastrophic realization that his frame of reference had been woefully inadequate. The new frame of reference called for quite different attitudes and behaviors.

I have told this story to many clients. I then add something like this: "I don't know exactly what the insignia is on your field cap. It might be, 'Human Being' or 'Child of God' or maybe something else. But I think the person you need to wear this cap for is *you* primarily, so that *you* can treat you properly. And maybe it's not enough to keep your field cap on the seat next to you. Maybe you need to wear it prominently on your head."

Much humor is this way. The beginning of the joke or story carefully builds up a particular world view, pointing to a particular conclusion. The punch line suddenly confronts us with a radically different world view that also satisfies the details of the story. But it does so in a way that we would not have anticipated.

Take, for instance, the story of the Turkish Sultan. He felt the foreign ambassadors were not showing enough humility as they entered his august presence. So he had the door to the throne room lowered, forcing those who entered to crawl in on hands and knees.

The English ambassador "rose" to the challenge. He crawled in backwards!

A good mystery story is similar to humor. The evidence seems to point to one particular conclusion. But in the end, a radically different and unexpected resolution is presented. If we had known the answer in the beginning, the evidence would have pointed even more clearly to the actual ending than the one we were led to expect.

First-century philosopher Epictetus said it well: "People are disturbed not by things but by the views they take of them!"

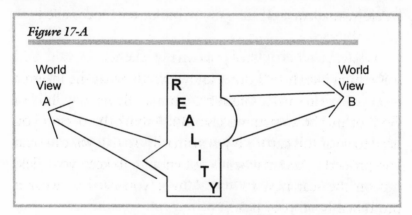

Figure 17-A

Figure 17-A illustrates the phenomenon in a graphic framework. "Reality" as seen from World View A is very different from the "Reality" viewed from World View B.

When people are disturbed, the world views that are implied by the events of their lives — the meanings they assign to these events — are distressing. They easily get locked into these destructive world views. A major part of healing and growth is for people to find other meanings in the events (inner and outer) of their lives. They can find other world views to shape their reactions.

We react much more to meanings than to events. If someone steps on my foot and quickly apologizes, the meanings in that event are not distressing. But if he steps on my foot and grunts angrily, "Get out of my way, Dummy," the meanings are quite different, as is my reaction.

In abusive relationships, an implied meaning is that you deserve to be hit, and I have the right to hit you. These meanings are often much more destructive than the physical damage. Professional boxers hit each other, and it does not seem to lower their self-esteem. The implied meanings are not humiliating. But when a man hits his wife, the meanings are devastating. Many women have said it took much longer for the psychological injuries to heal than the bruises and broken bones.

In a previous chapter, I pointed out that one's world view underlies everything that one does and is implicit in it. The corollary of this is also true: everything that one does implies a world view. There are deeper meanings to everything. Life being what it is, these deeper meanings are varied and complex. If you examine any behavior, you will find many levels of meaning and motivation.

Take the simple act of brushing one's teeth. A man may brush his teeth out of habit, to get rid of bad breath and a bad taste in his mouth, to help his teeth look nice and feel smooth, to appear attractive, to prevent cavities, to be loyal to his mother who made an issue of brushing, to set an example for his children, to feel superior to his brother whose teeth are terrible, as a spiritual discipline of caring for his body, as an obsessive-compulsive act, to validate his self-worth as one who is entitled to good health, and more. And this for such a simple thing as brushing teeth!

When we consider a much more symbolic area of life, such as eating or an emotional disturbance, the motivation is much more varied and complex. Each of these motivations implies a set of values, a world view.

Usually, we just do things without thinking about the motivations or implications. We accept the frames of reference that are most obvious. But when these obvious frames of reference are dysfunctional, we need to look deeper to find frames of reference that will promote healing and growth. This is a primary responsibility of the therapist, and reframing is one of the therapist's most powerful tools.

Reframing can come from many sources. It can be the result of new information, such as four stars on a field cap. It can come with the passage of time and the addition of new experiences. It can come from the deliberate interventions of a therapist.

One client was a thirty-eight-year-old recovering alcoholic, recovering sex addict, and recovering workaholic. An extremely sensitive and intelligent man, he is now a deeply spiritual person. As part of his therapy, he has reconnected with his parents, and found that to be both wonderful and traumatic. They have talked with him about how inadequate they were as parents and how they wish they could have been different.

This gave Stan a powerful affirmation of his perceptions of his childhood. But in a strange way it left him with an empty heart. He said that before this encounter, his heart was full of hate for them. With that gone, he just felt empty.

This plus several other changes left Stan feeling terribly agitated, anxious and depressed. He was so afraid he would kill himself that he would not spend the night alone in his home if his wife was out of town.

I said that one of the reasons he was so distraught was that he was in the midst of enormous change. Six months ago, he would have had no problem with all this. He would have found somebody to go to bed with, or gotten drunk, or immersed himself in some trivial project. Those ways of coping were no longer acceptable to him, so he was faced with the raw anxiety of change. I told him that his anxieties were a small price to pay for sobriety and health.

A middle-aged woman who was becoming increasingly depressed consulted a friend for therapy. She was not only worried about being depressed, she was especially anxious about not being in control of her feelings. The wife of a prominent doctor in a small Georgia town, she had recently finished raising her children and did not work.

At one point, David asked what her I.Q. was. When she said it was about 140, David told her he thought she was more bored than depressed. He elaborated on the challenges of raising children, which were no longer relevant for her. A person of her intelligence now needed something equally challenging. He proposed that she make a study of how women in a small Georgia town exercise power, and then report to him in a month.

On the surface, this appears to be a simple intervention, but it embraces several levels of meaning. First, his definition of her distress as boredom rather than depression implied a very different world view. Depression implies helplessness, pathology, inferiority. Boredom, on the other hand, as David defined it, implies superior abilities, normalcy, challenge. It is relatively easy to do something about boredom, whereas depression feels much more hopeless. Depressed people tend to be excessively oriented inwardly. David gave her an exercise that asked her to focus outwardly.

She was feeling immobilized by her depression. David gave her something to do, something that was well within her ability. He recognized her intelligence as a powerful asset and utilized that. Depressed people tend to be isolated from others. His assignment required that she mingle with people she knew. Depressed people usually feel powerless. David asked her to focus on the power of women. The question was not whether they have power, but how they use it. This implies a world view in which she as a woman has power and uses it. By attending to her power, she will give it reality and importance.

David said the client felt much better at the end of the hour. When he saw her the next month, she was feeling fine.

❖   ❖   ❖   ❖   ❖

Probably the best known example of reframing in the clinical literature came from Milton Erickson. Mrs. Erickson told me this was one of Milton's favorite case studies.

A twenty-one-year-old secretary sought therapy because, "I'm too inferior to live, I think. I've got no friends, I stay by myself and I'm too homely to get married. There's nothing for me but work and being an old maid; but I thought I'd see a psychiatrist before I committed suicide. I'm going to try you for three months' time and then, if things aren't straightened out, that's the end."

Her basic complaint was an ⅛-inch gap between her front teeth. She thought this made her impossibly unattractive, so she utterly neglected her grooming, her hair, her nails, and her clothing.

During the next few sessions, Dr. Erickson learned that she was intensely attracted to a young man at her work. She arranged to observe him when he went to the drinking fountain, but she ignored him and never spoke to him, even though he had made overtures.

Dr. Erickson then had her acquire some new clothing and get her hair dressed at the beauty shop. When she protested, he told her that since she was not optimistic about the future, she might as well have "one last fling."

He then focused on the gap between her front teeth. He had her learn to squirt water between this gap, until she achieved reasonable accuracy and distance. She regarded this assignment as silly and ridiculous. But she conscientiously practiced every evening "because it doesn't really matter what I do."

Dr. Erickson then proposed that she play a practical joke on the desirable young man. She would go to work the next Monday, nicely groomed and dressed in her new clothes. When the young man came to the drinking fountain, she would fill mouth with water and spray him. Then she was to giggle, start to run toward him, turn suddenly and "run like hell down the corridor."

When the young man exclaimed, "You damn little bitch," she laughed at him, and when she ran down the hall, he chased her. When he caught her, he declared, "For that kind of trick you're going to get a good kissing."

The next day, when she went to the drinking fountain, the young man squirted her with a water pistol. This led to another chase down the hall and another kiss, and an invitation to dinner.

Three weeks later, she told Dr. Erickson about these events. She said that the outcome of the silly prank had caused her to spend many thoughtful hours "taking inventory of myself." As a result she had one request to make of him. Would he coldly and honestly appraise her in detail. When this was done, she would terminate therapy.

Dr. Erickson discussed her original woebegone attitude, her unkempt appearance and her misconception that the ⅛-inch gap between her front teeth was a liability instead of an asset. He discussed her cooperation in therapy and the way she reacted to a pleasant event. She now realized she was an attractive woman, appreciated by a desirable young man.

This was the end of her therapy. Several months later, she sent Dr. Erickson an announcement of her engagement, and then of her marriage. Later still, he received a letter with a snapshot of her home, the announcement of her son's birth and a notice of her husband's promotion. Through the years, she referred several patients, all of whom spoke of her in glowing terms.

Gilbert was an airline pilot who had suffered through a terrible third marriage for seventeen years. Although rather naive, he seemed a truly good and gentle person. His first two marriages had ended very painfully, as had his parents' marriage. He was determined not to fail again. But his wife was a very paranoid woman who subjected him to verbal and sometimes physical abuse.

His first therapist tried to help him see his own part in the marital distress and ways he could cope better. Gilbert recognized the validity of this approach but ended up feeling even more depressed than ever. I focused more on the distress and helplessness he was feeling. At the end of the second session, I told him a story.

A pilot had been flying an airplane through a terrible storm for seventeen years. He tried everything he knew to escape this storm. He flew to the left and then to the right. He flew as high as the plane would go and then flew almost at ground level, but the storm filled the whole sky.

During all this time, the copilot criticized him for not doing a better job, and the passengers constantly complained about how rough the ride was. But nobody helped him with the responsibilities.

Finally after seventeen years, the plane was almost out of fuel. He knew he would never reach his destination. All he could do now was try to find some place to land in the storm without totally destroying the plane and everybody in it.

Gilbert nodded frequently during this story and seemed to be fighting back tears. A few weeks later, he began the process of filing for divorce.

Reframing is usually done straightforwardly, through verbal communications. It may also come through one's behavior or personal reactions, such as weeping. It may come through suggestions and directives. It may come through a story (metaphor) about myself or someone else, or even through confrontation.

There is a remarkable admonition by Jesus that is related to this. "If anyone strikes you on the right cheek, turn to him the other also. . ." (Matthew 5:39). Many people have read this as an admonition to accept abuse. I see it as just the opposite. I think Jesus was counseling people to take charge of the encounters of their lives — not to give up control.

If I hit you, I am defining you as an enemy. If you hit me back, you are accepting that definition. But if you do not hit me back, if you "turn the other cheek," you are taking charge of your own posture in the situation. You are being in control of you. You are saying, "I am not your enemy." This behavioral communication is perhaps the most powerful kind of reframing. It is much harder to lie behaviorally than to lie with words.

A friend woke up one night to see a man standing over her with a butcher knife in his hand. She said calmly, "What is it that you want? Do you want to kill me, or rape me, or rob me?"

He said, "No. I just want to look at you."

She asked him to put the knife down while she went to get a couple glasses of wine. She returned with the wine, and they talked for a couple hours before he left.

The man was surely defining the situation as one of threat, at least at first. But by her behavior, Hannah said very clearly, "I am not your enemy," and escaped unharmed. I don't think this reaction would be appropriate for every situation, or even for most situations. But on this occasion, her attitude served her extremely well.

Reframing can be directed to many purposes. Perhaps the ultimate purpose is the modeling that the therapist offers the client. If I as therapist can see things from several perspectives and see something worthwhile in everything, then the client can do that also, and learn to provide his/her own reframing.

This may be especially important in marital struggles, when one tends to see one's spouse in only one dimension. To be able to see other frames of reference can soften much conflict.

A teenage boy's parents complained that he seemed very alienated from them. The therapist suggested that maybe he was being very careful not to take sides in their conflicts. In another situation, a couple had separated because of their vitriolic arguments. Now that they were back together, the husband was not talking with his wife. The therapist suggested that maybe this was his attempt to improve relations, and he had not yet totally figured out how to do that effectively.

I tell people that a painful divorce is like a postgraduate course in self-understanding and human relations. They have paid an enormous tuition for this course. They should therefore learn *everything* they possibly can from it.

❖   ❖   ❖   ❖   ❖

Humor is often a gracious way to reframe. I remember a client who had hesitated to begin therapy. His friends had told him that *everything* was interpreted. His parents had been horribly intrusive, and he did not want to subject himself to the intrusiveness of unwanted interpretations.

One week he forgot his appointment! When he came the next week, he told me with great embarrassment about how he had agonized over the subconscious dynamics that caused him to forget. I wondered if this exercise on his part was to pre-empt my "judgement." If he explored his inner dynamics, I would not have the opportunity to.

But my wish was to help him create a world view in which mistakes can be taken nonchalantly. So I shook my head incredulously and said, "Foley, I'm really impressed at how much time and energy you've invested in trying to figure this out. The main thing I can say is that you've got a whole lot more leisure time than I do."

We laughed together. He then told me of his concern that I would explore things he didn't want to face. I told him that I had long ago given up trying to figure out why I did all the dumb things I did. I decided simply to forgive myself.

❖   ❖   ❖   ❖   ❖

A thirty-five-year-old mother of a delightful three-year-old boy had a terrifying phobia. For as long as she could remember, she had suffered from obsessions and phobias. Recently, she had been obsessed with fantasies of hurting her child. This is especially distressing because she thinks of herself as a really good mother. She has never hit (spanked) her child or even yelled at him. She could not understand these thoughts and fantasies and was concerned about being so abnormal. Wanda is active in her church and close to her husband, her brother, and a small circle of friends.

I told Wanda that I was impressed by the way she was raising her child. I don't believe in hitting children or yelling at them either. I thought her commitment to finding other ways to relate to him was wonderful. But the reality is that kids can be impossible sometimes. They often do things that really get their parents furious. They inevitably stir up angry feelings. That's just life.

Parents who don't mind yelling and hitting express those angry feelings by yelling and hitting. But she has made a commitment to treat her child decently. She has to do something else with those angry feelings. She is not going to act them out on her child.

Some people deal with those angry feelings by drinking too much or bitching at their spouses. Some get an ulcer or high blood pressure. It seemed to me that her angry feelings were taking the form of phobias about injuring her child. To my mind, that was perfectly understandable.

As a good parent, she does not yell and hit. But those angry feelings have to express themselves somewhere. With her, they express themselves in the form of phobias. I told her it was a small price to pay for being a good parent. I hoped she would remember that while we tried to find other ways to handle the frustrations of raising a small child.

Wanda's inability to control her thoughts and fantasies added greatly to her distress. But she also had two wonderful assets. She had a vivid imagination, and she had a circle of very close friends. So I told her that the next time she had these terrible thoughts of hurting her child, she should bring some other people into her imagination along with her. Bring in people who are gentle and strong, who *will not* let her hurt her child. Then no matter what terrible fantasies might come along, she need not be afraid. Other people are there to protect her.

I asked who some of these protective people might be. She mentioned her minister, her brother, her husband, me, and a few close friends. I suggested she bring the whole group. She might also bring Mother (who had been dead several years), Father and even God. When she had those terrible thoughts again, she could visualize all these persons standing around her and surrounding her with their love and strength and control.

There were three purposes to these remarks. First, I deliberately phrased it as, "The *next* time you have these terrible thoughts. . ." rather than, "*If* you should have these terrible thoughts again. . ." This was to give a sense of nonchalance to the presence of the thoughts. The important thing was not whether she was having the thoughts, but how she dealt with them.

The second purpose was to help her build ego strength by incorporating the characteristics of people who were important to her. All of us develop our sense of control by internalizing people who are important to us. In Wanda's case, the vivid imagination that created her problem also offered one means of its resolution.

The third purpose was to help give her a sense of control. She could not eliminate the unwanted thoughts, but she could modify them. That would effectively eliminate her helplessness.

Wanda left the office smiling and animated. A friend saw her at church the next Sunday and said she looked unusually radiant.

Marta was a sensitive vivacious nurse of thirty-two whose husband had committed suicide just three weeks earlier. He had put a pistol to his head and blown off a large section of his face and head. A major part of Marta's difficulty was a terror of seeing him walk into her bedroom or bathroom (the places she would feel the most vulnerable?) with the wound exposed.

I told Marta that the process of grieving, of saying goodbye, takes a long time, especially in such painful and complex circumstances as these. There is always an unfinished quality to any significant relationship. There are always things that need to be said that somehow didn't get said.

Her concern that Frank may reappear may be her subconscious mind telling her there is still some unfinished business that needs to be dealt with. If she were a visually oriented person, it would be natural for her to deal with this in visual terms, such as "seeing" him appear to her. That would be perfectly normal and appropriate.

I then asked if in her work as a nurse she had worked in surgery or plastic surgery. She had. In fact, she had a patient once with a wound very much like her husband's. She had no problems dressing the wound and changing his bandages. She also said that if Frank appeared with the wound bandaged, she could handle that. It was the thought of seeing him so disfigured that was so terrifying.

I told her that there are two special qualities that every nurse has to have. She has to be able to change roles easily, and she needs to be visually oriented. When she gets ready for work, she is in the role of person, wife, mother. But when she steps in the door to the hospital, she immediately assumes the role of nurse. She maintains that role until she leaves. I reminded her that she has had thousands of experiences of changing roles like this.

She has also had many experiences of creating images in her mind. These guide her in her work with patients. When someone needs a bandage, for instance, she has an image in her mind about how the finished bandaging will look. She has images of each step in the process. Those images are necessary for her to perform good nursing care.

If Frank appears to her without bandages, she should simply step into her role of nurse. She can tenderly and lovingly bandage the wound. Then she can step back into the role of wife and deal with the grieving process.

Since she is especially concerned about his appearing in the bathroom, she might deliberately visualize meeting him in some other room of the house. There are undoubtedly lots of things that need to be said to Frank in the process of saying goodbye. She might want to begin now to think of how she would say them.

I saw Marta briefly the next week. She said the terror about Frank's reappearing was gone, and she seemed to be getting on with her life better.

A woman whose husband had recently divorced her talked about how inferior she had always felt to him. The son of a successful businessman, he had been very popular in college as a leader, athlete, scholar, and all-around good guy. She never knew why he married her, since she always thought of herself as quite ordinary. A friend said of them once that Don was like a searchlight, and she was like a flashlight. This image seemed to be a focus of her low self-esteem.

I told her I thought that was a wonderful analogy. A searchlight exists to attract attention to itself, and you see them at sales events and sports spectaculars. A flashlight is simply used to find your way along in the dark. If I wanted a companion in life, I would much rather have a flashlight than a searchlight.

In the course of my work with Beth, I referred to this symbolism frequently and felt it helped with her growing self-confidence.

A colleague in Miami saw an elderly man whose son had committed suicide on his father's bed by taking an overdose of his father's medication. He and the boy had had a stormy relationship for the two years since Mom had left. Father felt that the suicide on his bed was a terribly hostile act directed at him. This, of course, made the boy's death absolutely devastating.

Elaine said that on the surface it may well have been a hostile act. But she wondered if under the surface this may have represented the son desperately trying to move toward him in some kind of way. At least in the moment of death, he wanted to be in a place where he could feel Dad's presence.

The father began weeping profusely, thanking Elaine for giving him some peace about the tragedy.

❖   ❖   ❖   ❖   ❖

I heard Carl Whitaker once talk about the beginnings of the style of therapy he and his colleagues developed. He and John Warkentin were in practice together at Oak Ridge, Tennessee back in the late 1940s. One day, Whitaker became intensely frightened of a violent paranoid patient. He excused himself for a moment to interrupt Warkentin. He insisted that John leave the patient he was seeing to come and sit in for the rest of the interview with the paranoid person.

As they walked back into Whitaker's office, Carl told the patient that he had asked Dr. Warkentin to sit in with them because he was afraid he (the patient) was going to kill him. Warkentin nonchalantly said, "I don't blame you for feeling that way. I've felt like killing him myself lots of times."

This comment drew a sharp line of distinction between feeling and doing. It gave approval to the feelings while making it very clear that you do not have to act on them.

When I was chaplain at a large state hospital, I worked with a suicidally depressed young woman. A few months after she was discharged, she wrote to tell me how difficult things were and how depressed she was becoming.

If I responded to the depression, I would have been giving reality to it. I would have been saying, "It is the depression that is important." Instead, I commented on how clearly she had communicated in her letter. That is very different from when we first met. I was emphasizing her ability to deal with her difficulties. She wrote back to tell me how much better my letter made her feel.

I have often told clients that their thoughts of suicide represent a determination *not* to go on living *this way*. It is their determination to find a different style of life. Divorce is often similar. The person is determined to divorce a particular kind of relating, to end the *kind* of marriage he or she has been in. This may or may not require a legal divorce.

❖   ❖   ❖   ❖   ❖

Lettie Mohammed directed a day treatment program for seriously disturbed mental patients. One woman was particularly troublesome because she refused to bathe. The staff constantly harassed her about this. When the staff could no longer stand the smell, they forced her to bathe and wear clean clothes. Crissy would meekly submit to the bath, but would put on dirty clothes under the clean ones.

Lettie saw how unproductive this power struggle was, and decided to take a different tack. She told Crissy that the only period in one's life when one does not bathe is when one is an infant, and a parent does it for her. She wondered if at some deep level, Crissy was asking the staff to realize that she really needed a lot of attention and tender loving care. She needed the kind of care a loving mother gives her little girl when she is bathing her.

Lettie told her that unfortunately, it would not be possible to give her that kind of bath. But if she liked, Lettie would be glad to give her a partial sponge bath every morning. She could let that sponge bath symbolize the kind of nurturing that every human being needs now and then. She offered to wash her hands and face, or one of her feet, or maybe a hand and arm, or maybe her face and neck. She could think about what would best symbolize the loving care that she seemed to want so deeply.

Lettie told me later that the nice thing about this intervention was that even if it was ineffective, no harm was done.

When I visit my grandchildren, I always tell them a bedtime story. One evening, I went into the bedroom and sat in the rocking chair. Lora, who was six, walked into the room, turned off the light, and got in my lap. A moment later, four-year-old Geri walked in the door, saw that the room was dark, and turned the light on and then off again. At this, Lora cried a kind of angry, protesting cry. She jumped up, ran to the light switch to turn it on and off herself. Then Geri protested.

I assumed that this was a regular conflict about who would get to have the final turn at the light switch. So I said excitedly, "Oh what an interesting game! One of you turns the light on and off, and the other cries! Now Geri, it's your turn. Go turn the light on and off, and Lora, you cry!"

Geri took her turn at the light switch, and Lora gave a kind of half-hearted cry. I gently criticized her crying, telling her that she could cry better than that. She tried again, but her heart was not in it. Then I said, "Now Lora, it's your turn. You turn the light on and off, and Geri you cry!" By this time, it was no longer a contest, but a game. Lora seemed a bit tickled as she turned the light on and off, and Geri laughingly tried to whimper.

I then said, "Now Geri, I wonder if you would like to take your turn by sitting in Grandaddy's lap and letting me tell you a story." She thought that was an excellent way to take her turn, as did Lora, and the conflict over the light switch was ended without either child losing face.

❖　　❖　　❖　　❖　　❖

A generation ago, many therapists operated on a kind of *energy model* of life. Things like instincts and feelings were psychic energies that needed to be directed and expressed. Colorful displays of anger, for instance, were called, "letting off steam."

An *information model* of life would understand things differently. If I yell at a friend, I may be letting off steam. But I am also commenting on the nature of our relationship. Gregory Bateson said that instincts should be thought of as explanatory principles rather than entities. Perhaps the same is true for feelings. They, too, may be explanatory principles rather than entities. To operate from this assumption leads to very different approaches.

An energy model would understand distressing feelings as being caused by something. "I am guilty because I did something wrong." "I am depressed because my child is leaving home."

An information model would think of feelings as being oriented primarily to the future. They are purposeful rather than reactive. "I feel guilty in order to remind myself not to do such and such again." "I feel depressed in order to remind myself to establish new ties with significant people."

A client one day was very discouraged. A very mature man, he had sought therapy to deepen his own sense of spirituality and had enjoyed some significant personal growth. But now it seemed he was regressing. He felt a mild depression and general feeling of malaise. He wondered what he was doing wrong.

I suggested that he think of these feelings as pointing to the future rather than to the past. Instead of looking into the past, he might look into the future. Maybe this was to remind him that there is effort involved in nurturing one's inner growth.

I then suggested he revisit in his memory some place that was associated with spirituality. Maybe it was a church, maybe a nature scene, maybe something else. Let him experience himself being there. Ask some of those questions that cannot be put into words. Experience answers which are felt in the heart rather than in the mind.

At the end of the hour, he felt much better and felt this approach was the correct one for him.

A rather shy young man consulted me because of his shame at dressing in women's clothes. He kept several items of clothing in his apartment and frequently wore them. I suggested this might be his way to incorporate some of the characteristics of his mother. She was obviously the strong one in the family, and Adam wanted to become more assertive. I thought this was an especially creative way to identify with Mother.

I suggested that he consider buying some inexpensive women's jewelry that he could carry inconspicuously in his pocket. Let the strength and assertiveness he associated with Mother slowly seep into his psyche.

Much later he told me he had bought a pair of earrings in a thrift shop and carried them in his pocket for many months. He occasionally wore a nightgown in the evening but no longer felt shame for it. He felt himself becoming stronger and more assertive.

18 ❖

Heart Attack
Reflections on the Tendency to Pathologize

Many years ago, a friend and colleague was rushed to the hospital with a heart attack. At first my other colleagues and I were stunned and sad at this unhappy catastrophe that had befallen Jonathan. But after discussing our distress and shock, our conversation slowly drifted to our recent contacts with him. All of these seemingly innocent contacts now took on an ominous significance in the light of the heart attack.

Jonathan had recently undertaken a new project associated with his work. We at first admired him for his creativity and initiative. But now we saw the obsessive nature of this overwork.

We had congratulated him for a particularly thorough report he had written. But we could now detect in it the manic qualities that would naturally portend a heart attack.

One of us had been at lunch with Jonathan and his wife, and everyone enjoyed teasing each other gently and pleasantly. Now on reflection, we could see that his teasing was in reality expressing a great deal of unexpressed tension and hostility.

One of his children had received an honor in school. We all had been pleased along with our friend. It was now evident that the child had been pushed relentlessly by a father driven to succeed.

The more we reflected, the more we could see the inevitability of the heart attack.

The next day, however, Jonathan unexpectedly returned to work! It had not been a heart attack after all, but only a severe case of indigestion. Several other customers of the same restaurant had suffered the same thing.

Suddenly everything was different! His obsessive overwork became once again merely creative initiative. His report no longer seemed obsessive, but only delightfully thorough. His "sinister" teasing became once again an innocent pastime. And a child succeeding in school was only a child succeeding in school.

It seemed that all of our gloomy prophesying had been nullified by the simple revision of a diagnosis, and we felt a little cheated. But as far as I was concerned, the matter was not finished. After all our hard work on his behalf, our friend now *owed* us a genuine heart attack, which we awaited impatiently.

H. Close. Originally published in *St. Luke's Journal* by the University of the South in March, 1972. (Renamed *Sewanee Theological Review*, 1991.) Adapted with permission of the publisher.

Metaphor and Rapport

*"What must I do to tame you?" asked
the Little Prince.*

Amiddle-aged mother of two children, aged nineteen
and twenty-one, slowly died of cancer over the
space of three years. The family reacted to this overwhelming
tragedy in a way that is not unusual. Each member lived out
his or her own style in an exaggerated manner. The father
had always been overinvolved in his business. Now he
became more involved. The son had been the rebel, caught
up in endless power struggles with his mother. This, too, was
now exacerbated.

The daughter had always been highly responsible and
nurturing. So the responsibility for shepherding mother
through the course of her illness was naturally assumed by
Maryann. She and her mother had always been close. Now
their closeness became almost a kind of psychological fusion.

Frances, the mother, had been extremely active in her
church, very close to the pastor as well as to many others.
When she died, she was cremated. Her ashes were buried in
an urn in the church cemetery.

187

Several days after the funeral, a woman strolling through the churchyard saw Maryann in the cemetery. She had unearthed the urn containing her mother's ashes. She was sitting there on the ground crying, holding the urn in her lap, stroking it and talking to it as though to her mother.

The woman was horrified at this and rushed to tell the pastor.

This pastor was a very wise man. He walked slowly to where Maryann was sitting and spoke to her softly. "Hello, Maryann." She looked up and nodded her acknowledgement. He said something about how hard it is to say goodbye. Maryann nodded again and continued to stroke the urn. He asked if he could sit with her. She nodded. He sat down and asked, "You've been talking to your mother?" She nodded.

He touched the urn also, just enough to affirm that this was an appropriate thing to do, but not so much as to take over the stroking. While his fingers were touching the urn, he, too, spoke as though to Frances. "I've missed you too, Frances. You were a good friend." There were tears in his eyes also. He then withdrew his hand and reminisced with Maryann about a particularly warm memory he had of her mother.

After some moments of silence, he told Maryann he would be glad to sit with her for a while. Or if she wanted some more time alone with Mother, that would be fine also.

Maryann said she would like some time alone.

He said a brief prayer and asked her to stop by to see him when she was ready to leave. He would be glad to rebury the urn or to help her rebury it.

When he returned to the office, he had his secretary watch the cemetery to make sure that Maryann was not disturbed.

A few minutes later, Maryann asked him to help her rebury the urn. He did so, with another brief prayer. He assured her that it would be fine for her to come to the cemetery any time she wished. He would be glad to help her in any way he could — either by being with her or by protecting her privacy.

Maryann thanked him warmly, and the priest felt this had been a very important part of the grieving process.

Maryann came to the cemetery frequently for a few weeks but apparently felt no further need to unearth the urn.

❖   ❖   ❖   ❖   ❖

To establish rapport, it is necessary to enter the other person's world and see things from that perspective. It is a function of the heart rather than of the mind. As such, it can best be established by using right brain processes. There are several things that seem to contribute to rapport, as illustrated in the following incidents.

In her reflections on her parents' lives, anthropologist Mary Catherine Bateson said that her terminally ill father, Gregory, went to a Zen monastery in San Francisco for his final days. As he lay in bed, the monks would take turns sitting beside him, breathing in synchronization with his breathing. Apparently this was an ancient Zen tradition, a way of supporting someone through the dying process.

To breathe in synchronization creates a powerful kind of rapport. I can do this if I speak a phrase while you are exhaling. We are then breathing together. Try it with your children the next time you read a bedtime story to them. As you near the end of the story, read more softly and more slowly, timing your phrases with their exhaling. One of

Dr. Erickson's children said of this approach, "Mommy talks us to sleep; Daddy breathes us to sleep."

You can try this with yourself if you have trouble falling asleep. Pick a number — say twenty — and count backward mentally toward zero. Synchronize this counting with your breathing. Think the first syllable of the number as you inhale, the second as you exhale. Part of the rationale for this is that breathing is a function of the subconscious mind; counting is a function of the conscious mind. When you have these two functioning together, it feels very whole, very secure, very relaxed.

Rapport can also be facilitated by mirroring a client's posture. Mirroring helps me to get into the client's frame of mind, into his or her feeling state. We all know that certain postures indicate certain feelings. If you are feeling depressed, for instance, you are likely to slouch forward with your head down, avoiding eye contact.

Postures also help *create* feelings. If I deliberately lower my head and avoid eye contact, I will begin to feel a little depressed myself. This will help me to resonate with your emotional state. It will help me to understand more deeply the world in which you live.

Mirroring a client's posture also communicates rapport at a subconscious level. I am confident that people pick up these messages and react to them. By mirroring a person's posture, I am communicating that in at least some obvious ways we are alike. We are in tune with each other, I am adapting to him or her. I am helping to communicate that I am not a threat.

I would want to do this very inconspicuously. To do otherwise would be a kind of mockery. But there are many ways of getting into the spirit of someone's posture without being noticed.

One man told me in the first session that his wife, who I would see the next day, was a slob. So before she arrived, I messed up my office a bit. I scattered papers on the desk, put the pillows on the couch in a bit of disarray and loosened my tie. If I knew a client was obsessively neat, I would make sure the office was as neat as possible. If I were to see a client who was deeply depressed, I would wear somber clothes.

Some therapists have set out to shock their clients by being radically different from them. If the client sat rigidly erect, the therapist might slouch down in his (I think only male therapists did this kind of thing) chair. He might even put his feet on a table. The therapist was showing the client how to relax and be less inhibited.

In my view, such an approach is extremely disrespectful. It ridicules and rejects the client's style and world view. How can I expect people to buy into my world view if I am unwilling to take theirs seriously?

A patient once asked Milton Erickson what he was doing with a bear trap in the middle of his office floor. I think Dr. Erickson suggested they both be careful of any traps that might be encountered anywhere (good advice for anyone!). At the end of the hour, Dr. Erickson carefully stepped around the imaginary bear trap!

You can mirror a client's behavior in other ways. If someone greets you with a limp handshake, you can make sure your hand is somewhat limp also. If the client is boisterous, you can be somewhat boisterous. With a stutterer, I will try to talk in a hesitant and uncertain manner, with lots of "uhs" thrown in.

❖   ❖   ❖   ❖   ❖

One of the most remarkable examples of speaking the other person's language comes from the work of Milton Erickson.

Harold was a manual laborer who walked hesitantly into Dr. Erickson's office. He stood in front of the desk and defined himself as, "I ain't very smart or much good. I don't never expect to be much good, but I ain't bad. I ain't nothin but a damn dumb no good moron, but I ain't never done nothin wrong. I work hard — see — them hands prove it. I got to work because if I stop I got to sit down and cry and be miserable and want to kill myself, and that ain't right."

After a few more comments, he turned dejectedly and walked toward the office door. Dr. Erickson waited until he had put his hand on the door knob, and was in a state of maximum receptiveness, before replying. "Listen you, listen to me. You're nothing but a miserable moron. You know how to work, you want help. You don't know nothing about doctoring. I do. You sit down in that there chair and you let me go to work."

To my mind, this was a beautiful and sensitive response to a man's anguish. Dr. Erickson had profoundly validated him and his world view by accepting his own definition of himself and speaking in his own language. After a few years of therapy, Harold had finished college and held a rewarding job.

A similar incident was reported by my friend Quentin Hand. While serving as pastor in a small New England town, he was asked to visit a friend's sister in the nearby state hospital. She had been diagnosed as catatonic schizophrenic and had been in the hospital for over a year, with not a single visitor for the past eight months.

Quentin began a series of regular weekly visits, always on the same day at the same time. Each time she was wearing a dreary hospital gown and robe, her hair unkempt. She watched him with a frightened gaze, and except for an occasional "yes" or "no," was absolutely silent.

"About the tenth week, this pattern changed. We sat again in relative silence as I would ask a question and wait for an answer. About twenty minutes into the visit, she looked at me in a sidelong way and said, 'You remind me of a song.'

"I was startled. This was the first sentence she had initiated with me.

" 'What song is that?' I replied.

" 'What a Friend We Have in Jesus,' Betty said.

" 'Did you used to sing that song in Sunday school?' I inquired. She smiled shyly and nodded. 'Would you like to sing it now?'

"This time she looked somewhat startled, but she nodded again. I began singing, 'What a friend we have in Jesus. . .' I continued the song for as many of the verses as I could remember. Betty would occasionally open her mouth and voice some of the words, looking at me for approval as she did so.

"I then asked what other songs she remembered from Sunday school. She volunteered a title, and I sang that one, asking her to join me. As we ended each one, I would ask for another. If she seemed unable to remember, I would suggest one which I remembered. For the remaining forty minutes of that hour, I sang and encouraged her to join me.

"The following week I called again on the same day and time. This time she was nicely dressed. She had been to the hospital beauty shop, and her hair was groomed neatly. She was wearing a bit of make-up, although she had not yet used fingernail polish. She greeted me with a smile rather than the frightened gaze of previous visits.

"She initiated the visit by saying, 'Hello.' It was the first time she had spoken first. She was not a conversationalist, but she made an effort to carry on an exchange. She told me about her eleven-year-old daughter and what she could remember of her admission to the hospital. The content of the hour was limited, but she was talking with me.

"I continued my weekly visits, with each week showing some slight improvement. About eight months later, she was released from the hospital, improved enough to care for herself and to be on her own."

A sensitive woman reported an incident with her four-year-old adopted son. The adoption agency had told them to make sure the word "adoption" was never a strange word to Rick. So they made sure he knew that he was adopted. They mentioned adoption frequently, they celebrated not only his birthday but also his coming-home day, and so forth. He really understood what it meant to be lovingly adopted.

When Rick was about four years old, Janice became pregnant. One day she was holding Rick in her lap when they both felt the baby kick in her womb. Rick asked his mother, "Mommy, did I kick like that when I was in your tummy?"

Janice said it nearly broke her heart to have to say, "I'm sure you kicked like that when you were in your Mommy's tummy."

When Janice told me this, she said that she was older now, and much wiser. Now she would understand this as an emotional question, not a factual question. Rick was asking, "Am I as important to you as the baby in your tummy?"

"I would know what to do now. I would hug him tightly and say, 'Yeah, I loved it when you were in my tummy.'" She would know that the word "tummy" meant "heart." She would have been communicating to him, in *his* language, "I have always loved the fact that you are in my heart."

❖   ❖   ❖   ❖   ❖

A prisoner of war wrote about the infamous Bataan death march in World War II.

"It was during a period of slow marching that an old friend, a captain in the medical corps, began dropping back through the ranks. Presently he was beside me. It was plain that he was just about done in. I said:

" 'Hello, Doc. Taking a walk?'

" 'Ed,' he said slowly, 'I can't go another kilometer. A little farther and I'm finished.'

" 'Well, Doc, I'm in the same fix,' I told him. Nothing more was said until we had covered two or three kilometers. Every now and then Doc would begin to lag a little. When this happened, the fellow on the other side of Doc would join me in slipping back some and giving him a little shove with our shoulders. He always took the hint and stepped up. At length he spoke again.

" 'I'm done, Ed. You fellows forget me and go on. I can't make another kilometer.'

" 'I don't think I can either, Doc. I feel just about as you do.'

"That was the way we passed the night. Kilometer after kilometer crawled by, but Doc didn't fall out. If he had, his bones would be bleaching now somewhere along the road of death that led out of Bataan."

If Ed had encouraged his friend, saying, "Come on Doc, you can make it," Doc would have *had* to fall out to prove how terrible he felt. By not reassuring him, but by identifying with him, Ed gave him the ability to go on.

One young man told me that he had many things he needed to say but was too timid to talk. So I asked him to write out the things he wanted us to think about together. This provided the structure for our sessions for several months. After a brief and uncomfortable exchange of greetings, he would give me his letter. I would read the letter aloud, interjecting comments and questions. The letter was something tangible to serve as the focus of our interaction.

If we think of rapport as speaking the client's language, and the client's language is writing or even silence, then it is important to be comfortable speaking it.

Sometimes the client's language is symbolic. When my father was in a nursing home in Miami, his concern about dying sometimes incorporated the symbolism of travelling. One day his pastor, the Rev. Riley Short, was visiting. Dad was rather agitated. Riley asked if something was troubling him. Dad said something about the train being late getting started.

Riley asked where the train was going.

"Chicago."

"Well, Kenneth, do you know anybody in Chicago?"

"No."

"You know, Chicago can get awful cold in the winter. You don't know anybody up there, and you have lots of friends here in Miami. I think it's probably a good thing that the train is taking so long to get started."

Riley didn't interpret Dad's symbolism. He simply entered into it and talked with Dad in Dad's language. I think this kind of support helped Dad to stay alive to celebrate his ninetieth birthday a few weeks later.

My friend Lettie Mohammed reported a similar experience with her father, a Navy veteran. He was in his late 80s when his health began to fail dramatically and he became rather confused. One day he was quite upset, saying he could not find his orders from the Navy that came in the mail the other day.

Lettie asked when he was supposed to report. He said he couldn't remember. She said he shouldn't worry about it. It would be a simple matter for the family to apply for a postponement of the orders. They could get a delay for as long as they wanted. That would give him time to get his affairs in order and say goodbye to everybody. The family wanted to keep him there with them for as long as they could. It wouldn't be any bother to apply for a postponement of the orders.

Her dad would also say he didn't want to be a bother to anybody. She would smile and tell him that everybody his age is supposed to say that. That gives the rest of the family a chance to fuss over them. "Besides, I was a bother to you when I was a baby. When you're not feeling well, that gives me a chance to take care of you, like you took care of me, and I like that."

❖   ❖   ❖   ❖   ❖

One aspect of rapport is trust. This, too, is a function of the heart and needs to be addressed by the languages of the heart.

A man was in a pool with a newly captured dolphin. At one point the dolphin swam up to the man, took the man's hand in his mouth and squeezed gently. The man took this behavior as part of the building of a relationship. He submitted to it, even though he knew a dolphin's jaws are strong enough to sever a man's hand in an instant.

The dolphin then swam around and rubbed his own neck — where the jugular vein would be — against the man's leg. The man interpreted the dolphin's behavior to signify that, "I could hurt you (by severing your hand), but I will not. I will make myself vulnerable to you (exposing my neck), confident that you will not hurt me." Perhaps this kind of mutual vulnerability is essential to any development of trust.

The question "Can I trust you?" is present in every client's heart. Until that question is answered, there will be little significant sharing. "Can I trust you to have my best interests at heart?" "Can I trust you to understand and accept me — not to laugh at me or to judge me?" "Can I trust you not to gossip?"

These questions cannot be answered directly. If I say, "Yes, you can trust me," that only arouses more suspicion. The harder I try to prove that I am trustworthy, the more suspicious you will become.

I've run across several approaches to the dilemma of creating trust. I prefer a straightforward approach: "You remind me of how sensitive I was to that question when I first saw a therapist." Or, "I've had people keep my secrets, and I know the importance of that." Or, "I remember how vulnerable I felt when I was in therapy and how concerned I was that my therapist might take advantage of that. I hope you will be as respectful of your vulnerability as you expect me to be."

Some responses are more elaborate: "I think the question of how trustworthy I am is something you will have to decide for yourself. You may want to wait a while before you decide to talk about really sensitive issues." Or, "I'm not out to make trouble for you. If there is ever any question in your mind about my confidentiality, I certainly hope you will talk about it with me." Or, "Some things may be relatively easy to talk about. Some things will be a lot harder to talk about. Why not postpone talking about those more painful things until you feel more comfortable." Or, "I really don't need to know everything about you. All I need to know are the things that will enable me to help you."

Occasionally someone will ask if the office is bugged. One therapist told a client that this was a legitimate question. He would help her search the office.

I sometimes record an interview so I can use that for my own growth as a therapist. But when I do, I have the microphone hanging from the ceiling, right in the middle of the room. It will then pick up our voices loudly and clearly so I don't have to strain to listen to it. It also communicates my commitment to being open and straightforward, rather than secretive.

When I was in training, I was required to present a weekly verbatim report. In my write-ups, I always doctored the conversations. I left out some of the dumb mistakes I had made. Like every other human being, I wanted to look good.

A few years later, supervising my own training program, I told trainees to feel free to lie on their verbatims. To the extent they thought I was out to get them or to embarrass them, they should feel free to lie. My wish was for them to learn, and they could learn as much from fantasy as from reality.

The only exception was if they blundered so badly that it would come to the attention of the administration. In that case, I needed a really accurate description of what happened so I could cover for them.

Several students have told me they were more honest with me than with previous supervisors, who had insisted that they be honest.

Rapport is not something that is accomplished and then forgotten. It is part of every contact with a person. The more agitated the client is, the more I need to attend to questions of rapport.

One woman was reliving the horrible trauma of being sexually assaulted as a child. As best as I could, I stuck to her like glue. She was speaking in short agitated phrases. I would repeat every one of them in a similar tone of voice. I altered the phrases just enough to let her know that I had assimilated their meaning and was not just emptily playing them back to her.

"I don't know who it is."

"You don't know who it is. He's a stranger."

"He's holding my arms!"

"He's holding your arms, and that's frightening."

"I can't move."

"You can't move, and you are trying so hard to get away."

❖   ❖   ❖   ❖   ❖

Speaking a person's name often is an important aspect of rapport and nurturing. There was an interesting experiment in a mental hospital in which all the patients were assigned randomly to various therapy groups. Leadership of these groups was then assigned to *all* the staff — psychiatrists, social workers, psychologists, chaplains, nurses, cooks, janitors and so forth. The sessions were taped and then evaluated by lay people.

Patients seemed to benefit from all these groups. In fact, I seem to recall that groups led by low status staff actually did better than those led by professionals. When the lay people analyzed the group interactions, they noticed one big difference: janitors and cooks spoke the patients names more frequently than the professionals did.

One young woman had been sexually abused by her father. One day she described a vivid dream she had the night before. She was about twelve years old, playing in her back yard. Suddenly her father appeared at the back door with a gun and started shooting at her. She changed into a dog and ran down to the creek where she saw me sitting on a rock. She jumped up into my lap and felt safe. When I addressed her by her name, she turned back into a person.

Nurturing is also an important part of rapport. There was a time when therapists experimented with nurturing people very directly. Some therapists would hold patients in their laps or even bottle-feed them. This was called reparenting.

I don't think this kind of thing is done much anymore. For one thing, the ethical standards of most professions strictly prohibit any physical contact with clients except a handshake. More importantly, this kind of therapy was not particularly effective. We now understand that the most effective nurturing is indirect rather than direct, symbolic rather than literal. No matter how well-meaning a therapist is, the client may feel it is contrived and artificial, or may suspect ulterior motives.

Perhaps clients associate direct nurturing with a kind of dependency that is not acceptable to many people. The message "I'll nurture you" may be like the message, "I'm trustworthy." It can be believed only if it is communicated indirectly. We nurture people when we give them our deep attention, our understanding, our feelings, our playfulness, our stories about our own lives.

Milton Erickson saw a young woman once who wanted to overcome her rigid inhibitions. Once she told him she wanted to get drunk. He told her that if she did this, she should lock the door to her apartment and put the key in a special out-of-the way place *before* she started drinking.

Later that evening she called him to say that she was delightfully tipsy and wanted to leave her apartment. Dr. Erickson reminded her that she was to keep the door locked with the key in an out-of-the-way place. That was essential to the experiment.

When she saw him again, she thanked him profusely for not letting her leave the apartment. She had wanted to find a man who would introduce her to sex. Now that she was sober, she realized she was nowhere near being ready for that. She deeply appreciated his protection.

Helping people save face is another aspect of protection. In any kind of therapy, you inevitably have to confront people with unpleasant realities of their lives. These psychological assaults can be tolerated only to the extent that clients feel your basic respect for them and your commitment to their well-being.

Implicit in your seeing them is the expectation of change. But nobody wants to change under what they may perceive as somebody else's pressure — even if they are paying you for that pressure. So the things we can do to help people to save face will make it easier for them to change.

Six-year-old Eddie was described by his mother as an angel in public but an absolute demon at home. He sat smugly and defiantly next to his father with his arms crossed as his mother described his behavior. He would yell, scream, throw things, and hit and kick both his mother and his eleven-year-old sister. The recitation of horrors was truly awesome.

I told Eddie I was really impressed that a six-year-old boy could do all those things. Unfortunately, I had never had an opportunity to see this in person. I wondered if he would give me a demonstration. Would he show me how he could yell and scream, hit and kick, and generally terrorize the family? I really would like to see this firsthand. Not so defiant now, he shook his head resolutely.

I then asked his sister if she would be willing to help Eddie. She agreed. I told her that I didn't think Eddie could really appreciate his performances. He didn't get to see himself do all the things his mother had described. So I asked Jane to pretend she was Eddie and show Eddie and me just how he looked and sounded. Eddie's expression had now changed to one of utter dismay. He crawled up in Daddy's lap and quietly sobbed while Jane gave her demonstration — a demonstration I am sure was a pale imitation of the real thing.

The next week, the family reported that Eddie had been much better. In fact, he had not really misbehaved at all that week.

I looked at Eddie. His smile was tinged with apprehension. I felt this was a crucial moment. If I commented on his improvement, I would be embarrassing him for the way he used to be. I would be the parents' ally against him. I needed to find some way to affirm his change without putting him down. Nobody wants to change under duress.

So I asked whimsically, "I wonder if you just kind of forgot to do some of those things your mom talked about last week?" He smiled broadly and nodded his agreement.

"You know, I forget things sometimes. I sometimes forget people's names. Did you ever forget somebody's name?"

Another enthusiastic agreement.

"And do you sometimes forget to come home on time, like to come home on time for supper sometimes?"

More agreement.

"And sometimes it is really nice to forget things. Like if you fall down and hurt yourself. Then after a little while you forget all about the hurt and go on playing. Did you ever do that?"

Repeated nodding, with a triumphant smile.

"But sometimes people don't always remember to forget. They *forget* to forget. If that happens, I'm sure Jane would be glad to help you again, to help you remember to forget. But if you remember to forget, she won't be able to help you at all. Won't she be frustrated then! I think Jane has been waiting all week long, just to help you to remember to forget. Won't she be upset if you have already remembered to forget.

And what is she going to do then?" These last words were spoken with serious and solemn emphasis.

"Eddie shook his head and said with absolute seriousness, "I don't know."

I wanted to neutralize the power struggle between Eddie and his parents. I equated behaving with forgetting — a neutral term. I could then wax eloquent about the virtues of forgetting, with no implied loss of face. Even I forget things sometimes, and sometimes it is nice to forget things. I was also giving him a new way to frustrate his family. He could frustrate Jane by behaving (remembering to forget) rather than frustrating them by misbehaving.

The family terminated therapy shortly thereafter for reasons unrelated to our work together. Eddie's behavior remained acceptable to his parents, but I do not know about the long-term adjustment of the family.

❖   ❖   ❖   ❖   ❖

A symbol I have used (based on a famous case study of Milton Erickson) is of a tree. In winter, the world around you becomes cold and dark. The life of the tree, the sap, withdraws from the world and seeks the safety and warmth of roots that are buried deep in the earth.

During the harshness of winter, nothing is asked of the tree but to survive. The leaves fall off, and the tree becomes barren and ugly. (Not everyone thinks a tree in winter is ugly, but the people for whom this story is told often *feel* ugly. I try to choose my words more for their effect than for their accuracy.)

But beauty is not called for in the winter. All that is called for is survival. There may be ice storms that break some of the limbs of the tree, leaving an open wound. But healing is not called for in winter. To all outward appearances, the tree is lifeless and dead. But growth is not called for in winter. All that is asked of the tree is to survive.

Finally in the beginning of spring, the days become longer, and there is more light than darkness. The harshness and cold of winter give way to the warmth of spring. In response to this light and warmth, the tree comes to life again. The sap is drawn by the increasing warmth of the world up through the trunk and out into the limbs and branches and twigs. Only then are healing and growth asked of the tree. But during the coldness and harshness of winter, all that is asked is to survive.

Guided meditation and hypnosis are often experienced as nurturing. I first learned this from two clients. The first was a woman who had consulted me for help with arthritis pain. One day we spent the entire hour talking about family matters. When I noticed that our time was up for the day, she asked me very disappointedly, "Aren't you going to hypnotize me today?" It was as though the hypnosis had a value to her all of its own, apart from the pain relief.

The other client told me that when I hypnotized her, it was as though I visited the child in her and brought forth optimism. I could not think of anything I had ever said that was directly related to optimism. So I concluded that the hypnotic experience itself created optimism — that it was nurturing.

I then realized that I did not use hypnosis with clients I did not like or respect. Hypnosis for me is an intimate way of relating to someone, and I am uncomfortable sharing that intimacy with people I don't like.

Frequently, clients will cry softly as they enter a hypnotic state, as though they are experiencing something that is tender and touching. When I do hypnosis or guided meditation, I give the client my intense attention. I speak softly in synchronization with his or her breathing. I often use metaphors or images that may well feel something like bedtime stories. All of these qualities add to the sense of nurturing that is implicit in the hypnotic experience.

20 ❖

Drama as Metaphor

I am using the term "drama" in this chapter in a very generic sense. It has to do with the crafted activities that a therapist suggests to or engages in with a client. This usage overlaps with metaphor and ritual, and the distinctions are often arbitrary. Drama is a kind of living metaphor and has all the power of metaphor plus the power of actually doing something.

The role of this kind of drama in psychotherapy has a long and honored history. Jesus, for instance, frequently instructed people to do things. He thus committed them to become actors in a kind of personalized drama. In the practice of prescribing penance, a sensitive priest could often create assignments with symbolic significance, engaging the parishioner's growth processes.

The priest or rabbi took on an active responsibility for the direction of healing and growth. He was like a theatrical director who created a kind of script for the parishioner and directed him or her in its performance.

But with the growth and prestige of psychoanalysis in the early part of this century, the models of psychotherapy shifted. An academic model replaced the dramatist model. The priest/therapist's role was seen as more passive in nature. He or she offered reflection and interpretation in the context of an empathetic and supportive relationship.

There was a kind of drama to this, of course. The interaction between the therapist and client was a kind of drama — sometimes a very moving drama. Each played a rather well-defined role. The philosophy was that growth takes place inwardly and then expresses itself outwardly. The therapist made clear (usually in indirect ways) that the principles of interaction there in the office were different from those of social interaction. This was a different kind of drama.

These were interactions that focused on one's inner life. By not getting involved in the client's "real" life, the therapist emphasized the importance of the office drama and the inner realities that were the focus of that interaction.

Milton Erickson was one of the first to break with this therapeutic tradition. In the 1930s, he was setting up dramatic situations for clients, often telling them to do things. As a result of the horrors of World War II, many combat veterans suffered from post-traumatic stress problems. Therapists often had the patient relive the situation — to reenact it as a drama.

Other therapies appeared which emphasized various kinds of drama as the focus of therapy. In group therapy, the group became the world in which people tried out new ways of relating. In family therapy, family members were often assigned therapeutic tasks, which were miniature dramas.

One of the most popular of the drama-oriented therapies was gestalt therapy, invented by Fritz Perls. Perls was born in Germany around the turn of the century. As a young man, he was enamored of the theater and wanted to be a theatrical director. His father, however, wanted him to be a lawyer. Perhaps as a kind of compromise, he became a doctor and then a psychoanalyst. He never lost his love for the theater. Eventually he created a very powerful therapy that embodied many of its principles. I encourage every therapist to become familiar with Perls's gestalt approach.

There are two different kinds of therapeutic drama: scenes staged in the office, and assignments to be performed elsewhere. These assignments are usually symbolic in nature and gently challenge an unproductive world view.

A very paranoid young woman said the people in her office were reading her mind and sending negative thoughts in her direction. I asked if she would like for me to put a shield around her. She agreed. I stood, made a big loop with my arms, and brought them over her head and all the way down toward the floor. I accidentally touched her arm and said I had to start over. It wouldn't work if I touched her. The next time was successful. When my arms were touching the floor I asked her to step out. She said that was great, and she felt much better.

I did this because it showed my support for her privacy and my wish for her to internalize some of my boundaries. I wanted her to find some way to exercise control over the situation. When I saw her a couple weeks later, she said the shield had lasted several days and then had begun to fade. But the situation wasn't so important to her anymore.

A woman was sent to a mental hospital because she kept hearing the voice of her dead daughter calling to her. I asked her one day when the last time was she heard Lola calling for her. She said it had been a couple of weeks earlier, in her room, standing by the window. So I went to the room with her and asked her to stand in the same place and listen very hard to hear Lola's voice. Her face showed that she was trying very hard. Finally she turned to me and said with deep pain, "She really is dead, isn't she?"

I nodded, and she began weeping — the first straightforward grieving she had allowed herself since her daughter's death.

❖   ❖   ❖   ❖   ❖

I think it is Albert Ellis who prescribes a terrifying ordeal for clients who consult him to overcome shyness. He has them take a ride on the subway. As the train approaches a station, the client must stand and announce the station in a loud official voice.

Milton Erickson was sometimes more personal in the ordeals to which he subjected shy patients. He might take the client to dinner in a nice restaurant and create an embarrassing scene that involved both of them.

Many therapists prescribe activities to couples. Couples who fight a lot might be told to schedule their arguments. Each can listen to the content of the other's concern instead of just listening to the anger and defensiveness. They might argue in a different place than they usually do — such as under the dining room table or in the bathtub.

Sometimes clients have been told to reverse roles in their arguments. If one usually criticizes and the other becomes defensive, they could reverse roles. It is hard work to be a critic, and conversely, the other needs to find out what it feels like to be on the receiving end of criticism.

Others have suggested that people argue by writing letters to each other. Husband writes to wife; she reads the letter in private, then waits at least two hours before responding. This might allow them to address the issues with less defensiveness.

Writing letters is often a very powerful kind of drama. A sexual abuse survivor was trying very hard to establish a relationship with her father. He had admitted the incest and apologized perfunctorily for it. She told him that she needed more than that. She needed for him to talk to her about that period of their lives. He asked her, somewhat irritated and sarcastic, what more she wanted. After all, he had apologized!. Did she want him to read a script?

She is afraid that he is empty inside. What she wants is some authentic, spontaneous comments that will show her that he takes his relationship with her seriously.

I told her to write a script for him to read. The words may be hers, but they may elicit genuine feelings. Ask him to read it two or three times. If it doesn't elicit what she wants today, ask him to read it to her again some other time. She should listen to the feelings she wants the words to convey. It is like a prayer of confession — an honored vehicle of the church. The words are given, and it allows the feelings to emerge.

I don't think self-esteem can be addressed directly. Any efforts to do so will trivialize the situation and make things worse. Perhaps the most direct thing you can do to enhance self-esteem is ask a question. "If your self-esteem were higher, what would you be doing that is different from what you are doing now?" If one starts living differently, then it is highly likely that one will start feeling different also.

Music can be a powerful life-changing intervention. In the church where my office is located, the choral soloist gives singing lessons. One day I impulsively suggested to a low self-esteem client that he take a half-hour singing lesson. He had been abused as a child, and I explained that this would help him get in touch with his body in a different way. It took some persuading, but he finally did. Here is an abridged account of his experience:

"When I walked into the room, I started feeling nervous and scared. Jennea made small talk with me in the beginning, and I chatted along with her. The more I talked, the more nervous I felt. I could not open my mouth. I felt paralyzed. I told her I was scared and afraid to hear my voice.

"A teacher in the sixth grade stopped the music class once in the middle of a song. She told me not to sing anymore since I was tone deaf. I have never sung anything since then.

"Jennea said no one will hurt me in here. She felt I could do it and it would be okay. We tried again. I opened my mouth but could hardly get anything out at first. I was hesitant, but I was able to make some noise as she played. I guess I was singing, but I thought it sounded horrible.

"After about four times singing 'Lu, lu, lu,' I told her I was really scared and felt lightheaded. She told me in a comforting voice that if I needed to throw up, there was a trash can next to the piano. I told her I heard all these negative voices telling me that I could not sing and for me not to do this. She said everyone in the world is basically scared.

"I tried again, and sang 'Lu, lu, lu,' four times. She said I was doing great, and I got a big smile on my face. Each time I tried, I felt better about letting my voice come out.

"I sang again, and toward the end I had made miraculous improvement. I actually could feel myself singing and heard my voice bouncing off the walls. This felt so freeing — a really new experience. Since the sixth grade, I have been scared to truly express myself. About that time I died in many ways emotionally.

"This singing was a big breakthrough. I felt my voice was trying to break through the walls of fear that have been built up through the years. It felt like the chains had been broken. I also felt I got in touch with my spirit, which had been locked deep inside me since the sixth grade. When I was singing, it felt like I was connecting to that deep spirit within me. I felt I connected to my long-lost self."*

Drawing on the work of Milton Erickson, many therapists have utilized a procedure called "prescribing the symptom." A patient may describe a behavior that is troublesome. The therapist may suggest the patient actually do the thing that is so troublesome, but do it in a slightly different way or in a different context.

A young couple consulted Dr. Erickson because they both suffered from enuresis. During their long courtship, neither had had the courage to tell the other about this affliction. After they were married, each thought the other unbelievably forbearing to accept the wet bed without comment.

Over the next several months, their love and devotion for each other grew immensely in appreciation for the

---

*Personal communication. Used with permission.

sympathetic silence about the wet bed. The secret came to light one morning when one of them said they really ought to get a baby to sleep with them, to explain the wet bed.

Dr. Erickson accepted them for experimental therapy on one condition: they must either benefit from the therapy or pay whatever fee he deemed appropriate. They solemnly promised to obey his instructions.

"This is what you are to do: Each evening you are to take fluids freely. Two hours before you go to bed, lock the bathroom door after drinking a glass of water. At bedtime get into your pajamas and then kneel side by side on the bed, facing your pillows, and deliberately, intentionally, and jointly wet the bed. This may be hard to do, but you must do it. Then lie down and go to sleep, knowing full well that the wetting of the bed is over and done with for the night, that nothing can really make it noticeably wetter.

"Do this every night, no matter how much you hate it — you have promised, though you did not know what the promise entailed, but you are obligated. Do it every night for two weeks — that is, until Sunday the seventeenth. On Sunday night you may take a rest from this task. You may that night lie down and go to sleep in a dry bed.

"On Monday morning, the eighteenth, you will arise, throw back the covers, and look at the bed. *Only as you see a wet bed, then and only then* will you realize that there will be before you another three weeks of kneeling and wetting the bed.

"You have your instructions. There will be no discussion and no debating between you about this, just silence. There will be only obedience, and you know *and will know what to do*. I will see you again in five weeks' time. You will then give me a full and amazing account.

"Five weeks later they entered the office, amused, chagrined, embarrassed, greatly pleased, but puzzled and uncertain about the writer's possible attitude and intentions.

"They had been most obedient. The first night had been one of torture. They had to kneel for over an hour before they could urinate. Succeeding nights were desperately dreaded. Each night they looked forward with an increasing intensity of desire to lie down and sleep in a dry bed on Sunday the seventeenth. On the morning of Monday the eighteenth, they awakened at the alarm and were amazed to find the bed still dry. Both started to speak and immediately remembered the admonition of silence.

"That night, in their pajamas, they looked at the bed, at each other, started to speak, but again remembered the instructions about silence. Impulsively they 'sneaked' into bed, turned off the reading light, wondering why they had not deliberately wet the bed but at the same time enjoying the comfort of a dry bed. . .

"A year later they introduced the writer to their infant son, amusedly stating that once more they could have a wet bed but only when they wished, and it would be just 'a cute little spot.' Hesitantly they asked if the writer had employed hypnosis on them. They were answered with the statement that their own honesty and sincerity in doing what was necessary to help themselves entitled them to full credit for what had been accomplished."

My friend Adrian Robinson once saw a janitor whose self-esteem was so low that he could not bear to look people in the eye. Adrian suggested that he do that deliberately for a while. "Try going a whole week without looking anyone in the eye, and see what you could learn from that experience."

The next week, the man said he was talking with one of the maids in the cafeteria and remembered about not looking anyone in the eye. So he kept his eyes pointed to the floor. He said it seemed as though the maid took her eyes and pried his eyes up from the floor. Before he knew it, she had made him look at her. He then thought to himself, "If I am good enough to look someone in the eye, I'm good enough to eat with them, too." For the first time in years, he sat down with some of the other staff to eat lunch.

One client was a kleptomaniac — she could not refrain from stealing things from stores. She told me one day she really did want to stop this. So I told her to bring me the next thing she stole. A couple weeks later, she brought a big bag of M & Ms and gave it to me with much embarrassment.

I then asked her to brag to me about her skill in stealing it. She was most reluctant to do this. But after some significant prodding on my part — and with great shame — she described the sequence of events.

I then gave her back the M & Ms. I told her, with much elaboration, I wanted her to replace it with the same skill and finesse with which she had stolen it: use the feigned nonchalance, the furtive glances, the supposedly casual movements of arms and hands.

She told me later that was the most difficult thing she had ever done in her life. As far as I know, this stopped the stealing, at least for the time we worked together.

Another client was referred by the police. I asked her to purchase duplicates of all the things she had ever stolen. She should then put them back on the shelves of the stores from which she had stolen them. Again, she was to use the same skill and finesse with which she had stolen them. I then told her that she needed to find some other ways to "lift" things.

I told her I was a "beach-lifter" — I collected shells from the beach. She might also try "salvage-lifting." In Miami, where I was living at the time, people would put their discarded furniture and so forth on the side of the street. It was picked up twice a week. Sometimes there were very nice things in these trash piles. I remember as a child bringing home a beautiful ornamental tree from somebody's trash pile. A young friend found enough parts to make bicycles for himself and his wife!

Sabrina took to this suggestion with obvious relish and soon was telling me of very interesting things she had salvaged from trash piles.

A rather different approach was used with an Episcopal priest. He was an ardent liberal who passionately loathed bigots. But he suffered from a compulsion to steal money from the petty-cash drawer at the church office. I said that when he was really committed to stopping this, when he was willing to do *anything* I suggested, to let me know.

A few weeks later he agreed. I told him the next time he stole money, to bring it to me. I would give half of it back to him, and send the other half to the Ku Klux Klan! He never brought me any money but told me later that this intervention had led to a gradual elimination of the stealing.

A young woman was afraid of driving anywhere. To help buttress her courage, she had filled her car with familiar things, especially stuffed animals. She had to make several trips to the car in the morning to carry out her entourage. There were similar trips in the evening to bring them back into the house. She was terribly embarrassed about this compulsion and the fears that lay behind it.

I told her that the primary way we learn things emotionally is to internalize the people who are important to us. In that way, we adopt certain characteristics of those people. All of us internalize things like confidence and courage in this manner. She was simply doing this belatedly and symbolically with the animals.

I asked if she had names for her animals, implying that she need not be ashamed of them. Does she have an animal named Henry, for instance? If not, why not name one of them for me temporarily. She might also take turns experimenting with leaving one animal home to guard the house. Maybe rotate the car duty for the animals. See how many are necessary to evoke her confidence; maybe have them sit in different places in the car.

Does she talk with them while driving? Or sing to them? If not, why not? Most of us have imaginary conversations while we are driving; why not with the animals?

I once asked if she felt safe in my office. She did, so I asked if there were something in the office she could take with her to symbolize strength and confidence while she was internalizing her own. She took a small polished rock and kept it for over a year before telling me she no longer needed it.

Wrist-cutting often occurs in a mental hospital like an epidemic. For a long while, no one will cut. Then suddenly several people will. Some cuts are superficial; some are serious. The cutting is usually on the wrist, although people have cut arms, legs, neck and torso. On rare occasions a person will literally cover the entire body with cuts.

Sometimes it seems like a chain of events. One person will cut, then another, and then another in rapid succession. Sometimes two or more people will get together and cut themselves simultaneously. These epidemics usually last only a short time before they die away for some weeks or months.

The efforts of staff to stop the cutting are usually ineffective. They embrace the whole gamut of techniques: punishment, sympathy, analysis, medication and/or shock treatment or transfer to another ward.

One afternoon I was chatting with a couple of young patients whom I did not know well. The girl's wrist was bandaged where she had cut herself the previous day. I told her I could understand that kind of thing. But cutting her wrist the way she did would not get at what was troubling her. People cut their wrists to try to drain off the poison that is in their hearts. But you can't drain it off by cutting yourself physically.

I told her I could cut her wrist in a way that *would* be helpful.

She consented, so I went to the nurses' station and returned with a red pen. I drew big red gashes on her other wrist, pressing hard enough to be uncomfortable, but not hard enough to break the skin. I asked her who had poisoned her heart by not loving her and by treating her badly. She said her mother and her sister had done that. I drew a large gash for each person and cross lines to connect the gashes, asking that she let the poison drain out thoroughly.

I asked her to tell me some of the things these people had said and done to put the poison in her heart. I then squeezed her arm in a downward motion, to get out as much poison as possible. I then asked whose appraisal of her as a worthwhile person she would like to put in her heart to take the place of the poison. Who would reassure her that she was a worthwhile person.

She thought for a moment and said, "God."

I affirmed that as a good choice and suggested she look around for other people who could also do that.

I told her I would be glad to cut her wrist again for her if the poison ever started building up. Or she could try this way of cutting her own wrist.

Sue was intensely involved in this whole procedure. She thanked me warmly and kissed me on the cheek — a rather remarkable gesture from a girl regarded by the staff as flippant and tough.

The young man who had been with us the whole time had scars on his wrist too. He wanted me to cut his wrist the same way I had cut Sue's. He talked reflectively about his abusive family as I drew cuts on his wrist. As I left, they both thanked me again.

That evening, they both walked me to my car to say good night. The next Monday morning, Sue greeted me warmly to tell me she had cut her wrist my way several times over the weekend. I had occasional contact with both of them for a couple of years. To the best of my knowledge, the wrist cutting had stopped.[2]

This incident occurred some twenty years ago. Since that time, many objections have been raised about any kind of physical touch between therapist and client. If I were to encounter a situation like this today, I would probably make it a fantasy exercise of some kind, rather than physically touching the client.

There are several reasons for prescribing behaviors that replicate people's symptoms. For one thing, it involves the therapist in this area of the client's life. It may then be easier for the client to internalize some of the therapist's personal characteristics.

By definition, a symptom is something over which the client has no control. To prescribe the symptom at least gives some measure of control — it alleviates the helplessness, which in itself can ease the pain of a symptom.

A very anxious client called one night in a near-panic to say she was shaking so badly that she could not sleep. I told her the shaking might just be excess energy. So I suggested she deliberately shake herself quite vigorously for a whole minute. If she still couldn't get to sleep, shake herself again for a whole minute — as often as necessary. When I saw her the next week, she said that two shakings were enough to enable her to sleep.

I remember a very disturbed woman who described everything in her life as hopeless. I asked and asked, but could find absolutely nothing that she regarded as worthwhile. Neither she nor I knew where to begin.

Finally I decided to coach her on the way she talked to her mother on the telephone. She could take charge of those conversations rather than just react!

Within a few weeks, Leah began to blossom. Within a few months, she had started a business course, was visiting her children and grandchildren regularly, and was also beginning to communicate with her husband.

I am convinced that her taking some action, especially in relation to her mother, helped her growth processes to get engaged.

Part of the power of drama is that it helps energize people. It is easy for one to lose initiative when things are going badly in life. To begin to do something purposeful again — even something "imaginary" — can be beneficial in and of itself.

Meditation and Fantasy

It's a poor sort of memory
that only works backwards.
— Lewis Carroll

A middle-aged woman was struck from behind while on the entrance ramp to the expressway. She had always been somewhat phobic, and this experience absolutely terrified her. Within a couple of weeks, she could hardly drive anywhere. In desperation, she consulted me for hypnosis to help her deal with the phobia.

Toward the end of our time together, I asked her to relax comfortably and let the insides of her eyelids become like a TV screen or a movie screen. This request implied that she would close her eyes. I reminded her of the split screen that is sometimes used in TV shows. One scene is presented on the left and another scene on the right.

I asked her to let herself remember an incident in her past that was characterized by feelings of confidence and well-being, by feelings of safety and security. Then play out that scene on the left-hand side of the TV screen. I elaborated on possible settings and sensations to make the scene become more alive for her. I then asked her to step into that scene and really feel those feelings of confidence and security, to let herself really relive those moments.

I then asked her to step out of that scene and let another scene play itself out on the right-hand side of the TV screen. This was the scene of the accident, and I asked her to step into this scene also. I then described the accident as catastrophically as I could, emphasizing her feelings of helplessness and terror.

After dwelling on the terror of the accident for some moments, I asked her to step out of that scene and back into the scene of comfort and confidence. Let herself really soak up those feelings of well-being.

I then took her back to the accident and described it again, this time somewhat less catastrophically. Then I took her back to the scene of safety and security, and then back to the scene of the accident.

This time I described the accident nonchalantly, in a very casual tone of voice. Then with a bit more animation, I pointed out that there were many more cars that did not hit her. Several people came to her assistance. There were buildings in the distance, with trees growing all around, clouds in the sky and a loving husband awaiting her at home.

The purpose of the double screen imagery was to help her integrate the dissociated traumatic experience into the normal fabric of her life. After all, all of us deal with trauma by gradually putting it in the total context of our living. This one session was apparently very helpful, for the accident was not discussed again in our work together. (This approach was suggested by a beautiful case study of Milton Erickson's, in which he helped his son Robert deal with nightmares that followed a serious accident.)

❖   ❖   ❖   ❖   ❖

Fantasy is one of the languages of the heart, and lends itself to a wide variety of therapeutic interventions. It is a kind of imaginary drama, with much of the power of drama to enhance one's inner growth processes. There is a kind of safety in this approach. One can deal with things inwardly that one is not yet ready to talk about. There is no loss of face.

Hypnosis is an excellent way to access this level of fantasy. I think every therapist should have at least some training in an Ericksonian approach to clinical hypnosis. If I am with a client who would be uneasy about that term, I will call it guided meditation. It is a state of altered awareness similar to daydreaming or being preoccupied. One withdraws attention from the external world and directs it to the internal world. One shifts from left brain dominance to a kind of right brain dominance, as one does when listening intently to meaningful music.

To help someone enter a hypnotic state, I typically shift my posture and look off into the distance for a few moments. I will speak in a quieter, more meditative and intense tone of voice, almost like a conspirator exchanging a message of immense importance. I may suggest that you close your eyes.

When eyes are open, there is an implicit demand for communication. I say something to you, and you will feel some kind of pressure to respond. Your response may be a nod or a "hmm," or it may be verbal. When a response is expected, at least some of your mental attention and energy is devoted to figuring out what you are going to say.

With your eyes closed, the situation is defined quite differently. No response is expected. You can let all your energies focus on what is said to you and how you can make use of that.

At the beginning of my talking, I will synchronize my phrases with your exhaling, as was discussed in the chapter on rapport. I will say something like: "I'd like to think out loud with you for a few minutes. And I would like to invite you to relax comfortably, . . . maybe (notice that the phrasing is permissive) let your eyes close, . . . breathe comfortably, . . . let your attention focus inwardly . . . "

I may then tell a therapeutic metaphor, or I may invite you to a fantasy exercise. If it is near the end of the hour, I may summarize what we have talked about and make some comments oriented to continued healing and growth. Only once have I had a client tell me this was not helpful, and many clients have said things that indicated the inward work was important and valuable.

For instance:

"During this hour, you have talked about something that happened to you many years ago, when you were just a little girl. In all innocence, you were down at the riding stable with your horse. This was one of the few things in your life that gave you a sense of belonging and made you feel important. While you were there, one of the young men approached you sexually and actually fondled you before you managed to get away.

"Like any little girl who has experienced that kind of abuse, you were embarrassed and humiliated. You were frightened; you felt like it was your fault. You felt you could not tell anyone because they might blame you. You have carried those painful feelings with you all these years, because you did not know how to deal with those painful feelings now.

"I would like for you to go back in time and relive that experience. You can take with you all of the many resources that are yours as an adult. You can take with you an adult's understanding of how a child must have felt. You can take an adult's feelings of indignation and support for that child. You can visit a child's experience with an adult's determination to . . . feel different about yourself.

"You can visit a child's feelings with an adult's love. You can visit a child's bewilderment with an adult's ability to learn from a situation like this. You can visit a child's helplessness with the strength and competence that are yours as an adult. As you visit that child's experience with the resources that are yours as an adult, you can . . . change the significance of that experience. Change the feelings that originated from that experience, and find ways to nurture and strengthen that child who still lives in your imagination. This child was terribly mistreated. You can take pride in knowing her and relating to her with love.

"The reality is that no one can always protect a child's body. You cannot always protect a child's feelings. Many terrible things happen to children that no one can stop.

"But you can surround the child's soul, that deepest part of her person, with your love. You can surround her soul with your protection, your love, your support."

A forty-three-year-old woman thought she had been sexually molested once. She was ill several months afterward and treated with an arsenic compound — the treatment for syphilis at that time. During her teenage years, she was very alienated from her parents, who would not talk with her about anything personal.

When, at age twenty-three, she told them she was seeing a psychologist, their horrified response was, "You can't do that to us!" Molly took that to mean that there was some horrible secret the family was afraid would be revealed. Even now, years after her parents have died, Molly feels ashamed and disloyal whenever she says anything uncomplimentary about them.

I invited Molly into a hypnotic state and told her, "Your mother and your father have been dead for several years now. Each of them has encountered God and has answered to God for the ways they lived their lives. The things they needed to acknowledge they, have acknowledged and have received an appropriate judgement. They have dealt with God about all the things they have done or not done. Where healing was needed, that healing has been accomplished now. Where forgiveness was needed, that forgiveness has been accomplished now. Each of them has made peace with God, with *whatever that took.*

"Your mother and your father can now face you as people who have been enlightened, and cleansed, and chastened. They have had to face all the realities of their lives, including the ways they treated you and your sister.

"I want you to visualize your mother and father standing in front of you now. Maybe they will put a hand lovingly on your shoulder as they speak. 'Molly, whatever you need to remember in order to accomplish your own healing, we want you to remember it. Whatever you need to say, even if it is about us, we want you to say it. We care now only about your well-being. Your well-being and your health are more important to us than our image. They are more important than how you feel about us.

" 'We have encountered God, and we are finally able to see things the way they really were, and we want you to do whatever you need to do to promote your well-being.' "

Molly wept softly while I was saying this, with a kind of disbelieving expression on her face. She then asked me to say it all over again, which I did. She then asked me to say it a third time, telling her clearly *what it was they said* (not, "what they *would* have said").

After repeating it again, I told her to take her own time to let that permission seep into her unconscious. She did not need to be in a hurry about remembering or saying anything. But she now had permission. After a short time of weeping and sorting through, she said her heart felt empty. The hate and bitterness were gone, and there seemed to be nothing in her heart where her parents used to be.

A woman in late twenties reported that she had been part of a satanic cult several years earlier and had done some really horrible things. Part of the brainwashing was to forbid her ever to talk about what had happened, or to write about it, or even to draw anything that might betray the secrets.

After several months of therapy, devoted largely to building a relationship of trust, the therapist suggested a fantasy exercise similar to the one described above. She told the client that there were many things that she might really like to talk about with someone, if she felt free to do so. If she felt really free, there might be some things that she could express in writing, or maybe even depict in a kind of drawing. In the privacy of her own thoughts, in the safety of her own thoughts, she could imagine what kinds of things she might say to someone, if she felt really free to do so.

What kinds of things might she say to her therapist, for instance? Or to someone else who really cares for you (notice the implicit message that the therapist really cares for her)? How might that person respond to some of the things she might say?

There are some clients for whom even this gentle approach might be too terrifying. In that case, the therapist might say it metaphorically. "I knew another woman once who had experienced some horrible things when she was younger and who felt that she could never tell anyone about them. Her therapist suggested to her one day that she might just imagine what kinds of things she might say if she felt really free to do so. . . ." This gives a little more distance, and can be important for certain clients.

There are some simple ways to suggest age regression or age progression. A fairly direct means would be to ask the client to visualize a calendar and then let the pages of the calendar turn slowly back to a point in the past. I personally prefer approaches that are more indirect. One is to build an emotional bridge between the present and the past.

One client described an encounter with her boyfriend in which she cruelly castigated him for some trivial offense. She knew while she was doing it that it was inappropriate, but she couldn't help herself. I asked her to get in a relaxed posture, close her eyes and gradually put herself back in that situation: "Let yourself feel again the terrible feelings of that moment — the hurt, the anger, the determination to hurt him. When you are feeling those feelings again, please let me know by nodding your head just enough for me to see."

After a few moments, she nodded her head. I asked her to build a kind of bridge, an emotional bridge, back to a time in her past when there were similar feelings, similar reactions. I told her to take her time, let the memories come without looking for them, to a situation where those feelings and reactions would have been appropriate.

After a couple of minutes, she said she was remembering very clearly a girlfriend she had as a child who constantly dominated her and put her down. As she talked about this painful relationship, she said she could see how sensitive she was to anyone treating her at all like this girl had treated her.

Another client said he had been waking up in terror the past few nights. I suggested he recreate the terror there in the office, and then build an emotional bridge back in time to a similar feeling in the past. Very quickly he remembered an experience at age seven when a cruel uncle had terrorized him by telling him his father had a mistress and his parents were going to divorce.

Edward was a man who was obsessively neat, especially about filing. His previous therapist had chided him about it, saying that this meant that he still needed a lot more therapy. He told me he had recently inherited some money and upgraded his ancient computer. He had had many things on old floppy disks — letters, poems, reflections, and so forth. He had now transferred these to the hard disk, complete with multiple entries and cross-referencing.

He said he had thrown away (erased) some old letters that expressed grievances with people. For a long time, it had been important to him to save these, but they now seemed unnecessary.

Toward the end of the hour, I suggested that his subconscious mind was like a gigantic hard disc, where all of the experiences of his life had been recorded. And now, in this time of growth and change, there are many of those memories that could be retrieved, revisited, reevaluated. Maybe some of those memories could just be erased — they were no longer relevant. Maybe others could just be enjoyed, as things that have made his life interesting and worthwhile.

Maybe some others could be put in a different file. Maybe there were some memories that had been put in the "Painful Memories" file, but that could now be put in the "Learning Experiences" file, or maybe in the "Dealing with Adversity Gracefully" file. A lot of memories can be refiled in some way or another. While I was talking, there were tears on his cheeks. Afterward, he asked enthusiastically that we do many more exercises like that one.

Sometimes a hypnotic state can help people cope with pain. A young man needed an arterial blood gas test. This is a very painful procedure. A needle is inserted between the tendons of the wrist to get blood from the artery.

During the first attempt, he broke out into a cold sweat with heart palpitations, which would have given a false reading. During the second attempt, he passed out. But he had to have this test.

I told him it was a simple matter to visualize things. It would be a simple matter to visualize a mannequin sitting next to him on the couch. The mannequin was about the same size and build as himself, dressed about like he was dressed, with the same appearance, the same way of combing his hair, the same posture.

It would be a simple matter to let himself merge with this mannequin, let his sense of self just blend into this mannequin. Become one with it, and really enjoy the peace and quietness, the relaxation of being totally passive, having no responsibility.

Now everybody knows that it is a simple matter to remove a part of the mannequin for a while to do something to it. You can take off a leg to put a shoe on. Then you put the leg back on, and the mannequin is complete again. Or you can take off the head to adjust the hair or the expression. Then you put the head back on, and the mannequin is complete again.

Or you can take an arm off. Put the arm on a table out in front of you. A nurse or a doctor may come along to do something to the arm. You can be very curious about the technique this person uses or what this person says while he or she is doing this procedure. You can be very curious about it all. Then when that person is through, it is a simple matter to put the arm back on the mannequin so that it is complete again.

You can enjoy the passivity and relaxation some more, for as long as you like. Then let your sense of self separate from the mannequin and merge back with your own body, taking with you only the benefits of this experience.

He called me the next week to tell me that the test had gone fine and to thank me for the experience. A few months later, I saw him again, and he referred to the blood test. He said the pain was just as bad as originally, but it had a totally different meaning. It was no longer frightening or intimidating.

I have had other people say things like that also. The meditation exercise did not take away all the pain, but it put it in a different context that was not terrifying.

A similar symbol is that of a marionette, with strings attached to all parts of the marionette's body, including the pain. The client is in complete control of all these strings. Then she can merge with the marionette, maintaining the complete control, and then let all the strings relax. After a period of really enjoying the relaxation, I will describe the process of putting an appropriate tension again on all the strings — but omit the string attached to the pain.

I often remind people that there are different parts of the mind that memorize different kinds of things. There is a part of the mind that can memorize numbers, such as the multiplication tables or someone's telephone number. You draw on those memories when you need them. There is a part of the mind that can memorize appearances so that you recognize a friend or the home in which you live. You draw on those memories when you need them.

There is part of the mind that can memorize sounds, such as the sound of a supportive friend's voice, or a piece of music. You draw on those memories when you need them. There is a part of the mind that can . . . memorize feelings, like feelings of comfort and relaxation, feelings of confidence and courage, the feeling of freedom from pain. And you draw on those memories when you need them.

Some clients have wanted me to use hypnosis to find out if they had been sexually abused as children. I always stress two things. The first is that healing can take place at a subconscious level, without a person having to know about it consciously. So it is not necessary to recover the memories consciously in order to experience healing.

The second is that if they recover no memories, it means one of two things. It may mean there was no traumatic event to remember. Or it may mean that your subconscious mind is not ready for you to deal with it. In either case, you need to accept the results as valid for you for the next period of your life. Wait for at least a year before probing your memory banks again. Maybe healing will have taken place inwardly so that you don't need to remember. Maybe your inner strengths will enable you to face whatever traumatic events there might have been. But for now, accept whatever you experience as appropriate for you.

I then ask the person to think of a scene that characterizes peace and security, a scene where one will feel totally safe and protected. For one woman, it was sitting on the couch next to Grandma, with her head resting on her shoulder. I asked her to visit that scene, relive it, put herself right there so she could be part of that scene again.

When she seemed to be there, I asked her to picture a VCR and monitor way off on the other side of the room. Next to it are many thousands of videotape memories of your life. You can glance at the titles and pick out a memory of a happy experience from your early life. Put the tape in the VCR, and take the remote back to the couch where you are sitting so safely with Grandma.

Now find out how the remote works. Play the tape at normal speed ,and then play it in slow motion. You can pause, or you can speed it up past certain places. You can play it with just the picture, with the sound turned all the way down. Or you can play just the audio, with the picture blacked out. She can play just the intellectual content, with the feelings turned all the way down. Maybe most important of all, you can stop it at any moment and play something else.

When you really know that you have complete control of the process, you can play the happy memory and really enjoy reliving it. You may then glance at another tape, maybe hold it in your hand a moment. You may then decide to put it back for now. Maybe pick out another tape and play it, knowing you are in control of that memory, safe on the couch with Grandma.

Maybe you will just catch a glimpse out of the corner of your eye of that memory that is playing on the monitor. If for any reason, it is too frightening, you can immediately turn your head away and feel again the safety and security of Grandma's presence. And at any time, you can simply turn the video off and tell yourself, "That's enough for today." The next day, you may want to repeat the whole sequence again, but maybe this time with the TV moved just a tiny bit closer. And whenever you wish, you can talk with me about anything you have seen or experienced.

Some people who enter very deeply into a hypnotic state do not immediately open their eyes when I am finished talking. A gentle way to help them reorient is to describe the process of waking up in the morning, with my voice gradually becoming more and more nonchalant, more and more normal.

"You know, different people have different ways of waking up in the morning. Some people like to open their eyes quickly and get on with the day."

I will pause now to see if the client is responding. If not, I will continue. "Other people like to wake up more gradually. Maybe just . . . (I will now speak these words so they sound like a suggestion instead of a statement) gradually become aware of background noises, like the noise from the street, or the sound of people talking in the next room. Or maybe . . . gradually become aware of the level of light in the room. Maybe . . . gradually become aware of a wish to stretch a little bit (here I will stretch myself and talk a little louder). Maybe take a deep breath, and then close your eyes tightly for a moment before opening them. Or maybe close your eyes tightly, and then take a deep breath before opening your eyes."

At this point, I would pause a few seconds and then begin talking in a normal nonchalant tone of voice about something related to the exercise. "It looked like you gave yourself a really nice experience," or, "How long did it seem like I was talking with you." I have *never* had anyone fail to respond to these simple techniques.

Therapy with a Dying Person

When a person approaches death, there are several themes that can be addressed helpfully by a therapist, pastor, and/or friend: normalizing the experience of death and accepting its reality, addressing possible guilt and shame, dealing with unresolved issues and relationships, entrusting the memories of one's life to loved ones, saying goodbye, letting go. As at other times in one's life, things like these are addressed more convincingly and with more power and grace if they are addressed metaphorically.

This is especially true of experiences of guilt and shame. If I tell someone, in my role as pastoral counselor, "All your 'sins,' (whatever that means for a particular person) have been forgiven," that will sound trite and insulting. But there are metaphors that can address that kind of thing powerfully and without insult.

I am reporting my work with one woman in some detail, as a concrete illustration of how I have used some of the principles and stories that are presented in this book.

Ellen was a member of the church where I am minister of counseling. She was a really exceptional and beautiful human being. I had known her and her husband well prior to the diagnosis of cancer. During the last months of her illness, I saw her weekly for supportive psychotherapy, using hypnosis and imagery. I would sit next to the bed, hold her hand and stroke her arm for a few moments (I would not have done this had we not been old friends), and then do a simple hypnotic induction and talk about things related to the process of dying.

I made sure my manner was straightforward and warm, rather than somber. I made a point of speaking her name frequently, which she said was particularly supportive to her. These were beautifully tender and intimate experiences for me. I felt she gave me access to a deep part of her soul, as I did for her. I am writing this report out of my deep respect and affection for her, as a way of finishing my own process of saying goodbye, and as an illustration of a metaphoric approach in counseling a dying person.

Ellen's world view was that of a conservative Christian, so I spoke from that perspective as sensitively as I could. I also made her an audiotape, in which I repeated many of the things I had said in person.

I sometimes began the early sessions with a variation of the following. I spoke slowly and softly, in very short phrases, and synchronized my phrases with her exhaling. If you will read this aloud, slowly and softly, you will get a better "feel" of what I was trying to convey.

"I would like to invite you, Ellen, to get in a really comfortable position, letting yourself take a couple of deep breaths, and relax quietly, letting your attention focus on the inner self, letting your subconscious mind be attentive to anything that can promote comfort and healing and strength.

"You may want to let your eyes close gently, or you may find that they will close all by themselves as we progress. There is no need to listen to me with your conscious mind, or even to be aware of my presence. To listen with the conscious self requires energy, and you don't need to do that. The subconscious mind can listen and understand without any effort, without any need to respond, without any expenditure of energy.

"You might want to give yourself a visual image of a place that represents healing and well-being for you, maybe a nature scene, maybe a beach at the ocean or a lake, with the colors of water and sky and background, the wonderfully invigorating sense of breeze and fragrance. Maybe it will be a mountain or a valley, maybe a garden or a stream, with all the sensations of color and pattern, the warmth of the sun on your face or the coolness of the breeze on your skin, the sounds of a running stream or of birds singing in the distance, and everything else that may accompany that experience, putting yourself into that place to feel its peace, its security, its healing."

Notice the different senses that were addressed: sight, sound, smell and touch. Notice also the permissive nature of all these comments. I never actually told her to do anything. By my tone of voice as well as through my words, I simply presented options and invited her to experience them. This approach to hypnosis was pioneered by Milton H. Erickson.

As the time arrived for me to leave, I would tell her that I was going to leave soon. She was welcome to keep my presence with her in any way she wanted. When I said goodbye, I wanted her to remain in a state of deep relaxation and peace. She did not need to say goodbye or acknowledge my leaving in any way. She could just continue to relax comfortably.

❖   ❖   ❖   ❖   ❖

On one occasion, I reminded Ellen that every stage of life has its own responsibilities, its own challenges, its own rewards. When she was an infant, she faced the many challenges of becoming more independent — learning to walk, to feed herself, to communicate, to relate to other children. As those tasks were accomplished, she felt a growing sense of pride and competence. I went on to review with her some highlights from each stage:

"As a teenager, you laid the foundations for your adult life, preparing for a career, choosing the partner with whom you would share your life. With these accomplishments came a growing sense of being your own person, able to make the important decisions about your life, and finding many moments of deep joy.

"As a young adult, you married and had three exceptional children. You invested yourself in the task of building a family — of learning to be a wife and mother, of enriching your own sense of being a loving person, of avoiding some of the mistakes your parents had made in raising you.

"In middle age, you came to understand God in a much deeper and more personal way, an understanding of the heart more than just the mind, and felt a deepening of your sense of being a truly spiritual person.

"As your children left home to establish their own careers and begin their own families, you gained a sense of being part of the broader flow of life, from father to son to grandson, from mother to daughter to granddaughter as one generation gives birth and meaning and purpose to another generation, and then another. You came to view yourself as an integral part of the whole fabric of life — not just your own family, but also the family of humanity.

"Now the final chapter is beginning to unfold. This is a time for stepping back and reviewing one's life. It is basically a time for reflection and celebration. To be sure, there are some other challenges as well: letting go of things that are peripheral, forgiving oneself and other people, saying goodbyes. But basically, it is a time for reflection and celebration. And in many ways, you have done that beautifully, setting aside time with your family to remember happy times you have shared together, and by the remembering, affirming and celebrating yourself and your life.

"There will be some specific memories of times when you were loved, of times when you really felt cherished and loved, maybe at a time when you might not have felt particularly lovable. But someone who was important to you saw beneath the surface and reached out to you in a beautiful kind of tenderness and affirmation. You felt an inner glow as you basked in the warmth of that person's love and appreciation for you. You felt good and strong inside. There may be a specific memory that comes to mind. As you relive that memory, you can put yourself again into that memory, savor its goodness, feel its power, know its deep meanings for you in the present."

I then told her about an epitaph that read, "I'm deeply grateful to God for the privilege of having lived." I thought that would be true for her and also for her family. They, too, would be grateful for her life.

On another occasion, I talked about the untold thousands of memories that are part of anyone's life, memories of many different kinds of things. "Many of these memories are happy, tender memories. Other memories may be sad, or even painful. It's like we have these memories filed away in our minds under various categories, almost like filing cabinets with different memories in different drawers.

"If someone asks me to recall a happy memory from the time my children were little, I can do that. I go to that drawer and retrieve a memory.

"Many of our memories can fit just as well in a different category than the one in which they were originally filed. During this final chapter of life, it is appropriate to revisit many of those memories, reevaluate them, and refile them.

"There may be a memory, for instance, of a terribly embarrassing incident. As you reflect on that memory, you may realize that your own embarrassment helped you be even more sensitive to other people's feelings. So that memory should be refiled under 'Helpful Learning Experiences' rather than under 'Embarrassing Memories.'

"Another memory may be of a time when you really treated someone shabbily, and you have carried a burden of guilt about that for a long time. As you review that memory, you may commit it to God. Then you can file it once and for all under 'Things for Which I have Been Forgiven' and let go of the guilt. Maybe a memory from the 'Stupid Mistakes' drawer can be refiled under the category of 'Experiences that Reminded Me of My Humanness.'

"During this final chapter of your life's drama, there will be many opportunities to review memories and make sure they are filed appropriately. You know that in the eyes of God, 'appropriate' means 'with love and forgiveness' ⎯

always. Because the ways of God are different from the ways of the world.

"In some ways, one's life is like a living portrait. Throughout the days of our lives, we keep adding a bit here and a bit there, every event eventually becoming part of the background. After a time, many of the events recede way back out of focus, providing a setting on which the foreground is built.

"Periodically the perspective of the portrait changes. You can see and understand the background and the processes differently. You also see and understand your own self differently. With each event in your life, you enrich this portrait, sometimes changing the focus, sometimes adding important new qualities, sometimes de-emphasizing one area so that you can highlight another.

"Not all of the pigments are bright and colorful. There are certainly many dark areas in anyone's life. Some of those dark times are of pain that had to be endured, 'valleys of the shadow of death' that had to be traversed. Some of them depict times of loss, of grief, of letting go. Some may represent mistakes that were made, maybe serious mistakes. But these mistakes ultimately helped you to choose more wisely the kind of person you wanted to be, the kind of life you wanted to live. So in that sense even those dark areas can be appreciated and celebrated.

"There are also many cheerful, joyful aspects to this portrait, many memories that still bring a smile and a deep sense of satisfaction. Each memory, each scene of the portrait can be thought of as a gift. Maybe the gift was an affirmation from a friend or loved one. Maybe the gift was something that led you — or maybe pushed you — to a deeper sense of your own inner self. Maybe many other kinds of gifts of the spirit that cannot be named or described, but can only be accepted by the heart.

"Some areas of the portrait are clear and precise; others are more diffuse, nebulous. Some learnings may have been harder to come by. But now you can step back and review the whole painting. You may look at one incident that is part of the background, smile warmly and think to yourself, 'I'm so grateful for that.' There may be another incident in which you really felt good about what you said and did. You can say to yourself, 'I hope my family and my friends never forget that.'

"There may be other scenes that are part of the background of that portrait. Some are of times when you really felt loved, when someone or maybe more than one person truly and deeply loved you, and you felt blessed. There may be other scenes in which you felt very close to God. You were in touch with your own spirituality and felt a sense of wholeness, of being at peace with yourself and the whole world, where you felt an authentic joy in the depth of your soul.

"As the closing pages of this final chapter approach, it is time to say goodbye. You can visit in your imagination many of the places, the events, the things, the people that have been important to you, and say goodbye to them with warmth and appreciation.

"There may be special places you have always enjoyed being — maybe a room in your home, maybe a church, maybe a place you have visited on vacations — that hold some very special memories for you. You can visit those places again in your imagination. Let yourself experience again the pleasures of being there, and with a warm smile, say goodbye to those places.

"There may be some certain things that are very special to you, maybe a tree you planted in your yard, maybe a gift someone gave you, maybe something one of your children made for you, maybe something else. Take that item into your consciousness now, let yourself appreciate it anew, maybe imagine yourself touching it and saying, 'Thank you for the pleasures you have brought me,' as you say goodbye.

"There are certain events that live in your memory. You can put yourself back into those events, experience them anew as you say your goodbyes. And, of course, there are the people who have been important to you and to whom you have been important. You can let yourself do a leisurely review of many of those people who have been part of your life. There may be something special you will want to say to each one of them in your goodbyes, something special each of them will say to you, maybe in words, maybe even more so in the expression on their faces or the warmth of their embrace.

"Finally there may be some special things you have said or done that seem to capture the essence of the 'you' that you want people to remember. Take some time to revisit those special moments. You can smile as you look into the future to a time when your husband is remembering a time that you and he have shared, and breathes a prayer of gratitude for you. Or you can take great pleasure in visiting a time in the future when one of your children remembers something about you and smiles to himself or herself and says, 'I'm glad I had a mother like that.'

"So this final chapter of life has its own unique responsibilities, challenges, opportunities, gratifications. When the time comes for that chapter to be closed, you entrust the memories of yourself, the 'portrait' of your life, to the loving care of your family, and entrust your Self to the loving care of God."

When I worked in a mental hospital, I saw a patient who had suffered a number of terrible losses in recent months and was profoundly depressed. Toward the end of our work together, she said that at the beginning she felt as if she were trapped in a room with a huge piece of ice blocking the door. She would rub on the ice with her hands to try to melt some of it away. But she could only rub for a little while because her hands got so cold.

She would leave the ice and do some other things for a while, rubbing her hands together to get them warm again. Then she would go back to the ice and rub some more. Finally she had melted away enough of the ice so there was a hole big enough for her to crawl out of.

I told this story to another woman who was finally coming to grips with the fact that her father had sexually molested her when she was a child. When she asked her friends what she should do, she got a variety of answers. One friend told her to forget about it and get on with her life. But she knew that pretending would not make the block of ice go away.

Another friend told her the exact opposite. This had to be her number one priority, and she should put everything else in her life on hold until she had dealt with this trauma. But she could not bear to face that humiliation for very long at a time. Her friend was, in effect, seizing her hands and trying to hold them against the ice perpetually — which cannot be done without serious damage.

I told Ellen about these people, and continued.

"Unfortunately, Ellen, your friends cannot rub the ice for you; nobody else has access to it. But what your friends can do is help you get your hands warm again. They can hold your hands gently against their heart, to let you feel their love for you."

Ellen interrupted me to say, "As you are doing for me." I nodded, "Yes, as I am doing for you. I'm holding your hands lovingly next to my heart to help them to get warm."

❖   ❖   ❖   ❖   ❖

In March, Ellen had been told she had a month or so to live, maybe two at the most. She very much wanted to live through June, when her oldest son would graduate from medical school. It was a great joy when she attended the graduation. Then she wanted to live through July, when a son who was a missionary in Japan would be able to visit. That, too, was a happy gift for her. Then she wanted to live through September, when a daughter in Hawaii would give birth to her first granddaughter. But holding on was getting harder and harder.

One day early in September she told me she had had a terrible two weeks. I told her that the time would come when she would want me to talk about letting go, just as in the past she had wanted me to talk about holding on. She told me she thought that time was coming very soon. I asked if she would like me to talk on this day about letting go. She nodded.

I took her hand and stroked her arm, as I usually did. Speaking very slowly and softly, I then took her on an elaborate imaginary trip to visit the daughter in Hawaii. I talked about how the ocean is the womb from which all life has come, and how appropriate that the islands of Hawaii are surrounded by the ocean. I pointed out the changes in the color and texture of the ocean as we flew over the reefs, the beauty and power of the surf as it crashed against the rocky coast, the beauty and majesty of the mountains in the distance.

"When we land at the airport, we are met by your daughter and son-in-law, who drive you to their home. You can take particular pleasure in the beautiful flowers you see along the way (Ellen loved flowers) — flowers and trees and shrubs that are very different from those here in Atlanta: orchids, bromeliads, antheriums, hibiscus, all a glorious burst of color and design and splendor. The trees are different too, different shades of color, shapes, textures, leaf formations, all speaking of the tremendous goodness and variety of life.

"You can also be interested in the beautiful birds you see and hear as you drive through the neighborhood. Hawaii is known for its spectacular colorful birds and their beautiful singing, and it will be like they are singing just for you.

"When you arrive at your daughter's home, you will greet your two grandsons, who adore you. You will enjoy a wonderful afternoon with the whole family, reminiscing and celebrating your life together. Then later on, it will be time to go to the birthing center. Your daughter's husband will stand on one side, and you on the other, holding your daughter's hands as she gives birth. She has a very easy delivery, so you can devote your whole attention to the beautiful little girl who is being born.

"I don't know whether you will look first at your daughter — and the pride you will feel for her and the joy you will feel as you see her joy — or if you will look first at the baby. You will surely notice everything about her —

whom she looks like, the color of her hair, how she wiggles her hands and feet, what kinds of sounds she makes. Your own mother once looked on you with that same sense of mystery and awe, as you yourself have done with your own daughter.

"Baby will be washed and given to your daughter, who will hold her warmly for a while. Then she will give baby to her husband, who will hold her in his own special way. Then he will hand baby to you. You will hold baby warmly next to your own body, to let baby feel the warmth of your body and the pulse of your heart, and hear the sound of your voice. You will feel a tremendous glow of love radiating from your heart as you hold this new life in your arms. You may even be aware of tears in your eyes.

"You will know you are surrounding this baby not only with love and warmth, but with the deepest qualities of your soul. You will bestow on baby a kind of blessing that cannot be put into words, but that baby will know, and will feel, and will keep with her for her entire life. You have a special gift to give her that no one else can give — the gift of courage in the face of hard times. By the way you have lived these past few months, you have proclaimed that no matter how hard life is, life is worthwhile.

"Like any other human being, baby will have some hard times to go through. But she will go through them with a deep-seated realization that she carries the blessing not only of her parents, but in a special way she carries the blessing of grandmother for her first granddaughter, a grandmother who has modeled courage and determination. You can feel yourself loving and blessing this child, planting the seeds of those values and perspectives that have sustained you throughout your own life.

"After a little while, when you feel the blessing has been fully bestowed, it is time to give baby back to her mother, and for you to step back with a deep satisfaction. Your life has now had a wonderful culmination, a wonderful fulfillment, and it is all right to let go.

"As you begin to let go, you can be aware of the people who have gone before you, and who will be waiting to greet you. (I emphasized this because research has shown that most rituals surrounding the processes of dying focus not on the bereaved, but on incorporating the dead person into the community of life that is beyond death.) Father will be there, along with your grandparents. They have been waiting for you for a long time.

"There will be other people there who have been important to you. Your brother will be there, aunts and uncles who may have been special to you, maybe cousins. There will also be friends there — your roommate from college, maybe a neighbor, maybe a pastor — people who have meant a lot to you in the course of your life, and people to whom you have meant a lot. They will especially want to greet you with their love and appreciation.

"I don't know how you will envision God and Jesus greeting you, but they will be there too. And then you can look forward to greeting the friends and loved ones who will come along later. They will all be along in due time. Mother will be there soon. Then your husband before too awfully long. I'll be there before too long and will really look forward to your greeting me. And you can know that it is all all right, that your life has come to its own beautiful conclusion. You have been privileged to be part of the flow of life from one generation to another, and now it is all right to let go.

"So you can now picture yourself flying back home. At an appropriate time, you may lie down in bed, call your husband and children and grandchildren — especially your new granddaughter — to come and be with you. Maybe they will sit on the bed and hold your hand or caress your arm. You will tell them that you are ready to go now, and you entrust your life and your memories to them in loving appreciation. Then you might just say goodbye, and close your eyes quietly, and let go."

When I told Ellen's husband about this (and later about another) imaginary trip, he seemed particularly touched.

The next week it was obvious that death was near. I told her how glad I was that she had had the opportunity to visit her daughter in Hawaii and be there for the birth of her first granddaughter. I summarized the trip and then talked with her again about saying goodbye and letting go.

I saw Ellen again four days later. Her husband said she had wanted to visit her mother one last time — she was an Alzheimer's patient in a nursing home in the small town where she had grown up. But Ellen was far too weak for any kind of trip. So I took her on another elaborate imaginary trip to visit them.

I described the familiar drive through the serene countryside, pointing out as many of the features as I could think of, including a sailboat on the lake next to the highway. As we came to the house in which she had grown up, I asked her to notice the trees and flowers in the yard. Notice the familiar look of the house, the furnishings, the pictures on the wall, the smells emanating from the kitchen, maybe even a familiar creak of the floorboards.

Mother and Dad are both there, in good health, in full possession of their faculties. She will greet them warmly and reminisce about happy memories they shared together. Then she will say her loving goodbyes to them. She will look forward to seeing them again soon in another life.

I then described a leisurely and pleasant drive back home, which she enjoyed with the deep satisfaction of having said her final goodbyes. I then talked at some length about her dying with a smile on her face, a smile in her heart, knowing how many smiles she had brought to other people.

As I said goodbye and started to leave, she opened her hands toward me, indicating that she wanted me to hug her. As I did, she said with great effort, "I love you."

It was only after I had left the room that the moisture in my eyes became tears.

Three days later she was in a coma. I repeated some of the things I had said to her earlier, confident that the subconscious mind still hears and registers what is said. That afternoon, her granddaughter was born in Hawaii, two weeks early. Her husband held the phone to her ear so she could hear her granddaughter's "voice." A few hours later, she died quietly.

A concert pianist once said that a musician does not memorize his music — that would be impossible. A piano concerto may have as many as 500,000 notes. There is no way anyone could memorize that. Instead, he takes the music into his soul, lets it become part of him, enriches it with his own personal qualities. Then in a performance, the music "sings itself through him."

My time with Ellen reminded me that this is true of psychotherapy also. Therapy is not a "thing" to be dispensed, like aspirin, even if that therapy consists of great wisdom, sensitivity and warmth. Psychotherapy is a particular kind of relationship between persons who, at least to some extent, open their hearts to each other. Most of the things I said to Ellen were unplanned. When I walked into her room, something came to life between us, and the words then sang themselves through me to her.

H. Close, "Pastoral Care for an Unconscious Person." Some of the material in this chapter appeared in this article. Originally published in *The Journal of Pastoral Care,* Summer, 1998. Used with permission of the publisher.

In loving memory of Ellen. Her family has read this chapter and agreed to its publication. This material was presented as a seminar at the Sixth International Congress on Ericksonian Approaches to Hypnosis and Therapy, Los Angeles, December, 1994.

Part F

Concluding Considerations

Symmetry and Complementarity

I have been rereading Gregory Bateson recently — a daunting undertaking. Bateson was a man of monumental learning, embracing several different fields. He was undoubtedly one of the great minds of our century. But his work is not easy to understand. I am often left with the sense that he is saying some really important things. I just wish I could figure out what they are!

I gather that I am not alone in finding Bateson difficult. One of his colleagues, Jay Haley, said that Gregory often gave the impression that if you understood what he was saying, he felt he wasn't being profound enough.

Gregory Bateson (named for Gregor Mendel) was the youngest of three sons of William Bateson and the only one to live to adulthood. The senior Bateson is generally recognized as the father of the science of genetics.

Gregory became an anthropologist. In 1937, he wrote a groundbreaking study, *Naven*, in which he introduced the concepts of Symmetry and Complementarity. Then in 1942, he wrote a fascinating article, "Morale and National

Character" (reprinted in *Steps to an Ecology of Mind*) in which he elaborated on these concepts.

In 1962, Haley referred to these in his revolutionary book, *Strategies of Psychotherapy*. In 1967, Paul Watzlawick, Janet Bevin and Don Jackson discussed them at some length in *Pragmatics of Human Communication*. Then in 1971, Bateson wrote another seminal article, "The Cybernetics of Self: A Theory of Alcoholism" (also in *Steps to an Ecology of Mind*). But I have seen little in contemporary literature about these concepts of symmetry and complementarity — which puzzles me greatly.

I hope this chapter can help regenerate some of the interest I feel these concepts deserve.

A *symmetrical interaction* is one in which the participants exchange similar kinds of behavior. Each person's behavior stimulates more of the same kind of behavior from the other. I insult you, you insult me, and then I insult you some more. I tell you my problems, you tell me your problems. I tell you about my achievements; you tell me about yours. I withdraw; you withdraw. My country builds bombs; your country builds bombs. A symmetrical interaction emphasizes the equality of the two participants.

This kind of interaction can go on unchecked. It easily becomes competitive, with each party striving to one-up the other, to be quantitatively better than the other.

My friend Bob Myers once told me about a rather impressive boat he had built. Without really knowing what I was doing, I immediately told him about a project I had recently completed. I was affirming our equality! Another friend told me that he had run across an article of mine in some journal, and then immediately told me at some length that he had recently been quoted in *Time* magazine.

One variation occurs when I respond defensively to an accusation. The accusation is felt as competitive, an effort to put me one down. My defense is an affirmation, "We are not unequal; your putdown is not justified."

Another variation has to do with retaliation. "You have put me down. I cannot rest until I have gotten even [a wonderfully descriptive phrase] by putting you down."

In a symmetrical interaction, if I apologize to you, you will minimize the offense. "I'm sorry I bumped into you." "Forget it." Symmetrical interactions emphasize similarities and minimize differences.

A *complementary interaction* is one in which the participants exchange different kinds of behavior. The behaviors fit together, with each presupposing the other. Each person's behavior stimulates a matching kind of behavior from the other. Each person plays a role in relation to the other's contrasting role. I insult you; you cry. I tell you my problems; you give me advice. I brag about my achievements; you compliment me.

These interactions emphasize the structural differences, inequalities, between the participants (actually, between the roles they are playing) while they are relating in this mode. This is the interaction between mother and child (you can't be a mother without a child), boss and employee, teacher and student, officer and enlisted person.

When a complementary interaction escalates, it leads to an increasing rigidity and polarity of the roles the participants play.

In a complementary interaction, one person's role is in a sense one-up; the other's is one-down. But this is a different use of the terms "one-up" and "one-down" than in a symmetrical interaction. There, people strive for a *quantitative* superiority: you are one-up because you scored more points that I did in our game (using the term "game" in its broadest sense). In a complementary interaction, the differences are *qualitative* rather than quantitative. You are one-up because you console me for my ineptness.

It is unfortunate that all the terms describing a complementary interaction imply a personal, social or moral superiority. This is in no way implied in these concepts. If you can think of better terms than "one up" and "one down," please let me know.

❖   ❖   ❖   ❖   ❖

Naturalists have observed two male wolves vying for dominance. They snarl, bare their fangs and lunge toward each other. Finally one will submit by lying on the ground and his exposing his neck. At this sign of submission, the winner walks away.

This is obviously a symmetrical interaction. When one is aggressive, the other is also. When one backs off, so does the other. This is rather different from their interaction with caribou. When the caribou submits, it is eaten.

A motorist picked up a hitchhiker, who later murdered him. When the killer was apprehended, he said the victim pleaded for his life. But the killer just laughed at him, enjoying his humiliation before killing him.

The victim was in a subordinate, one-down position. But the more he played this role, the more he stimulated the dominance and aggression of the other person. If the victim had been nonchalant in his relation to the hitchhiker, perhaps he could have survived.

When Iraq defeated Kuwait in 1990, they brutalized the country. They tortured and killed civilians, looting the country and destroying its facilities and resources. During World War II, the Japanese, Germans and Russians were also brutal to those they defeated. The one-down position of the victims stimulated even more dominance on the part of the victors.

The United States is a more symmetrically oriented culture. We treated prisoners well and then helped rehabilitate the defeated countries.

Bruno Bettleheim was in a concentration camp during World War II. One day he suffered from frostbite and needed medical attention. He knew that prisoners with medical problems did not often get help. So he studied the requests of the men ahead of him in line for treatment. They tended to adopt a one-down submissive stance. They would tell of their pain or how they had sacrificed for the Fatherland in World War I. None of these ploys worked.

Bettleheim simply stated, unemotionally, that he suffered from frostbite. He could not work effectively without medical attention. He got the treatment he needed.

The words, "I love you!" are often spoken as a request (or demand) for a symmetrical response: "I love you too." But this response is often unconvincing because it is in a sense forced. A complementary response might regard those words as a loving gift, which calls for acceptance and appreciation rather than reciprocity.

❖   ❖   ❖   ❖   ❖

It is interesting to note that the philosophy of nonviolent social protest has been effective only in cultures that value symmetry. Martin Luther King, Jr. in the United States and Mohandas K. Gandhi in India were effective in their protests. The Jews were nonviolent in Germany and were engulfed in the Holocaust.

During a time of horrible rioting in India, Gandhi let it be known that he would fast until the rioting stopped. From one perspective, he was putting himself one-down. But from that stance he exerted tremendous power. His acceptance of the one-down position enabled those who admired him to step out of their own horrible competitiveness. They surrendered their aggression, and the rioting stopped.

A good *relationship* needs to have all three kinds of interactions: symmetrical (we each talk about our experiences of the day); complementary, with you in a one-up position (you nurture me when I am depressed); and complementary, with me in the one-up position (I teach you how to use the computer).

When any one style escalates in an undesirable way, someone needs to create a graceful transition. If a conversation becomes excessively competitive, one can ask advice from the other. If an interaction is excessively complementary, one can introduce symmetry, maybe in the form of playfulness.

In a good marriage, the symmetry can be thought of in broader terms. In addition to many areas of straightforward symmetry, I am dominant in some areas while you are in other areas. Also in a good marriage, the transitions are graceful rather than catastrophic — such physical abuse or drunkenness.

It is unfortunate if a person gets locked into or out of any one position. A man who *cannot* let his wife mother him when he's sick misses an important balance in his marriage. Some parents just *cannot* take advice about raising children, yet cannot stop *giving* advice to their children.

A rather tyrannical father had so badgered his youngest son that the young man hated him. Father was approaching parenting from a complementary posture, while the son wanted the relationship to be more equal. Finally the young man's life fell apart as he lost his job, his wife and his children. In desperation he asked father if he could come home.

From that point, they began to build a much better relationship. The young man could no longer maintain his side of the competition. He accepted a complementary one-down posture with father, around the axis of nurture rather than dominance. If the boy could have done this earlier, or if the father could have moved toward equality, much grief might have been avoided.

A friend told me that his wife often said she felt inferior to him. This was astonishing to me, since I knew both of them. His assurances to the contrary fell on deaf ears, and he was concerned about whether she would leave. I pointed out that when you reassure someone, you are inevitably stepping into a one-up position. You are thereby reinforcing the very thing you are trying to negate.

The only thing I thought would work would be for him to adopt a one-down stance with her. He might remind her that he was an only child and had spent his whole life on a pedestal. When she felt inferior, that meant he had gotten up on his pedestal again. Instead of telling him she felt inferior, she should shake his pedestal. He would fight her tooth and toenail, of course, but ultimately would appreciate her effort to humanize him.

These terms refer to *interactions,* not individual behavior. A man can undertake to dominate someone. If the other accepts the dominance, then the interaction is complementary. But if the other responds with dominant moves of his or her own, the interaction is symmetrical.

Of course, nothing in life is as simple as I have described it. There are often deeper levels of symmetry in many complementary interactions, and vice versa. I teach a client some important truths about life, but the client pays me for this service. So in one sense, I am one-up as a teacher and one-down as a hired hand. I teach you how to sail a boat, and the next day you teach me about the British history. A woman (or man) is severely depressed, but from that one-down position, she may effectively control the rest of the family.

The complexity of the roles and interactions may make it impossible to make sense of them from these perspectives. This may be especially true in healthy families, where these things are not issues and roles are held loosely. In troubled families, it may be easier to see things from these perspectives.

If one spouse defines the interaction as symmetrical and the other wants it to be complementary, there is going to be a great deal of tension. Adolescents frequently want relationships in which their parents meet all their needs (complementarity) and also give them total freedom (symmetry). This is rather the opposite of what the parents want of their children. They want the kids to take care of their own needs and also abide by parental restrictions.

In his 1942 article ("Morale and National Character"), Bateson discussed at length three areas of complementarity: dominance/submission, succorance/dependency, exhibitionism/spectatorship. Other areas might include sadism/masochism, aggression/passivity, jealousy/provocativeness, possessive/possessed and others.

In various cultures, these themes are woven together with differing degrees of emphasis. One observation was particularly interesting to me. In England, it is the parents who are the exhibitionists, the performers. By their behavior they show their observing children how to go about being adult.

In the United States, it is the children who are the performers. They show their parents how they are becoming progressively more independent. Bateson observed that when an Englishman (perhaps it is different for women???) does something that is exhibitionistic (such as lecturing or delivering a sermon), he is functioning like a parent. His concern is, "Did I contribute something worthwhile?" When an American lectures or preaches (or writes a book, like this one), he steps into the role of child performing for parental approval. His concern is, "Did I look good?"

Much is being said nowadays about spirituality. But this is a very difficult concept to put into words. Spirituality certainly has little to do with channeling, past lives, runes, crystals, reincarnation or exotic Chinese or Indian procedures. Nor is spirituality compatible with competitiveness ("I am more spiritual than you!" or, "My guru or my religion is better than your guru or your religion!" or, "My spirituality has enabled me to succeed in business!").

Perhaps the essence of spirituality is experienced in a complementary approach to life and to that which transcends life. It is a sense of awe at the mysteries of nature and the meanings of life. It is a sense of joy in response to beauty or tenderness, a grateful acceptance of what is. Perhaps it is enhanced when guilt is transmuted into humility, anger into determination, humiliation into awareness, depression into acceptance.

Ultimately, that with which one enters a complementary relationship may need to be experienced as personal. It may not be necessary to believe in God. But it may be essential that one experience that transcendent reality as personal. As a sensitive client said, "It is clear to me that I love God; it is not all that clear that I believe in God."

In the middle ages, the reverse tended to be true. Everybody believed in God, but it was difficult to associate love with God.

In Islamic cultures, religion may be experienced as highly complementary, around the axis of dominance and submission. Arab cultures in particular are characterized by sharply defined social hierarchies, including the submission of women to men and children to parents. Maybe spirituality for a Muslim has to do with complementarity around a different axis than that of dominance/submission, such as succorance/dependency. Perhaps it is to gain a sense of equality, of shared responsibility.

Forgiveness may be one expression of this — an attitude of minimizing differences between people. Jesus alluded to the sense of equality when he said to a Semitic world that a *man* should leave his father and mother and be joined to his wife. It is difficult for us today to understand how incredibly radical these words must have sounded.

I had an interesting experience in Japan. I led a hypnosis workshop there, attended by a few European therapists as well as some from China and from Japan. At one point, a German psychologist said he would feel very uncomfortable giving a suggestion to someone who was in a hypnotic state. That would feel manipulative.

This was a very thoughtful humanistic statement from someone who understood hierarchies in terms of power. He did not want to take advantage of someone's vulnerability. In the Prussian tradition, to which we Americans are heir, hierarchies are understood primarily in terms of power. Someone of higher standing has the authority to tell one of lower standing what to do.

But the Japanese understanding of hierarchies has another dimension. Alongside the orientation to power is a profound sense of responsibility to protect and to nurture. So I asked one of the Japanese participants, "If someone gave you a suggestion when you were in a hypnotic state, would that *feel* manipulative to you?"

"Oh no, it would feel like he understood me and really wanted to help me."

It is interesting to wonder if a Zen philosophy could thrive only in a culture that understood hierarchies in this manner. Perhaps the moment of insight is not so much an internal event as it is a shift in the interaction between student and master. The student no longer accepts a one-down position.

❖   ❖   ❖   ❖   ❖

Bateson's article on alcoholism ("The Cybernetics of 'Self': A Theory of Alcoholism") is very interesting. He suggests that the alcoholic gets locked into a horrible competitive (symmetrical) struggle with the bottle. One may "win" for a while. But the very nature of competitiveness makes one keep on playing the game forever. If one wins today, one must take up the challenge again tomorrow. Ultimately, this pathological symmetry becomes intolerable, and one flees to the comfort of a complementary interaction. He or she surrenders to the bottle.

The horrible tension of unabated symmetry has led inevitably to an extreme act of complementarity. So getting drunk is a cure for the pathological competitiveness with the bottle.

Bateson then says that the genius of AA is that it offers an identical kind of complementarity — total surrender. But that surrender is to the program rather than to the bottle. The AA program duplicates the structural experience of being drunk (surrendering). It then expands that to a complementary approach to all of life. All the things in the AA program reinforce this complementarity. There is surrender to God, confession, reparations, anonymity and the mission of carrying the message of AA to the world.

Bateson goes so far as to say that anything competitive might be hazardous to a recovering alcoholic — even a game of checkers or tennis.*

I am concerned that the efforts of legislators to "get tough on drunk drivers" will simply raise the stakes of the game. It may make it more challenging and therefore more interesting.

---

*Bateson does not relate this way of thinking about alcoholism to our understandings of codependency. For me to try to do so is beyond the scope of this chapter.

The shift from symmetry to complementarity (or vice versa) might be an example of what Watzlawick, Weakland and others have called *second-order change*.

I have asked several recovering alcoholic clients and friends about this concept. They all affirmed its accuracy. One new client actually used the phrase, "competing with the bottle" in the very first session. Other addictions have this same competitiveness also — overeating, smoking and so forth. They need the same "cure" of entering a complementary relationship with life.

One client had been trying to lose weight for years. Finally one summer she made a profound commitment to her religion. Immediately she felt that she could lose the weight she wanted, and she succeeded fairly easily.

In one experiment, people were shown a subliminal message, "Mommy and I are one!" This simple intervention has helped people to stop smoking, lose weight and so forth.

This reminder of a primitive complementarity seemed to help people step out of a competitive relationship with the addiction. They could then adopt a one-down dependent posture related to nurturing. For very religious people, the message might be, "God and I are one," or for some committed Christians, "Jesus and I are one."

I heard Carl Whitaker say once that psychotherapy was impossible for an atheist. This is finally making sense to me. An emotional atheist does not put himself or herself one-down in relation to life and to the broader mysteries of life. *Psycho*therapy — the healing of the soul — requires something of this kind of complementarity.

One client was a very sensitive and intelligent recovering addict. After a while, I found myself impatient with his constantly putting himself down. I would gently suggest that he might want to view himself differently. He was totally resistant to these suggestions.

This was about the time I started rereading Bateson. I suddenly realized what my client was doing. He was determined to live from a complementary posture rather than a symmetrical one. It did not matter how much personal discomfort that entailed. My efforts to treat him as an equal were from this perspective a threat to his sobriety!

Therapists often try to alleviate people's guilt. But this guilt may be an important embodiment of their complementary approach to life. To remove it may be disastrous. Although I would try gently to let the guilt transform itself into humility, I now understand that unfortunate consequences might result from trying to remove it.

If I feel that pathological symmetry is a main problem, I can make sure my relationship with the client is complementary. I may nurture (hypnosis is often very nurturing), gently dominate (confront) or evaluate his/her performance.

I can suggest things that will reinforce the complementarity. The very act of suggesting comes from a dominant one-up position. The content of the suggestion may be irrelevant. Some very peculiar things seem to have helped people. If the client follows the suggestion, it may be of value simply because of this aspect of the relationship.

Much marital conflict is symmetrical in nature. Sometimes it seems that the primary purpose of the conflict is to affirm the symmetry, the equality. If I point out what is wrong with you, you will point out what is wrong with me. If I blame you, you will blame me — even if just to blame you for blaming me. Or if I attack you, you will defend yourself.

This sequence often goes on until one person resorts to violence or leaves. These responses are very unhappy shifts into complementarity.

Consider what might happen if the "contestants" were to shift to a different kind of symmetry. If I point out what is wrong with *me* rather than what is wrong with you, the underlying symmetry would pressure you to do the same. If I apologize, you may apologize. This would be like one wolf exposing his neck to the other.

Consider the case of a couple whose twelve-year marriage had grown increasingly conflictual — a dreadful symmetry. They had already failed with two therapists and were increasingly angry at each other. They could not divorce because of family, social and religious pressures — or perhaps because divorce would seem like losing.

One possible intervention might be a fantasy exercise in which the therapist would ask them to close their eyes and visualize a drama taking place in the office. They could flip a coin to see who went first.

The wife, for example, might imagine her husband kneeling before her, saying, "I know I have been very hard to live with. I deeply regret all the mean, petty and thoughtless things I have done and not done." She would be asked to imagine what she might do in response. Then they would swap roles and repeat the procedure.

The therapist would then ask them to leave the office in silence and spend the rest of the day meditating on the learnings this exercise might hold for them.

If a couple could accept a suggestion from the therapist, that in itself might help break the horrible symmetry. And the language of fantasy might be effective where other languages have failed.

❖   ❖   ❖   ❖   ❖

Depression, phobias and paranoia are obvious examples of pathological complementarity. At a feeling level, the person is one-down, powerless, even though this stance exerts tremendous power over other people. A shift to more symmetrical interactions may help bring healing.

Introducing symmetry and equality would be a first priority. I might present myself as a friend, a joke-teller, a fellow sufferer, a competitor, or as one who will engage him or her in play. My stories and my reframing would emphasize equality and competence.

A woman who had her therapist on a magnificent pedestal was alternately depressed and furious at his "superiority." If he confronts her or analyzes her attitude, he is adopting a one-up posture, which reinforces the complementarity. Instead, he might tell her about his own therapy — even if he has to make up some of the details:

"You know, you make me think back to when I was in therapy, and how unrealistically I used to think of my therapist. As far as I was concerned, he was vastly superior to me. I had a lot of trouble with that for a long time. I remember how hard it was for me even to look him in the eye. But I think I learned some valuable things from that experience. I think I'm a lot more sensitive to people's feelings now than I used to be."

Helen had fought against depression for years. She had spent many months in a state hospital as an adolescent.

During most of her adult life, she struggled with a sense of personal inadequacy.

One day she told me of a series of traumatic events. When she went for her annual physical examination, a lump was discovered in her breast, and the doctor recommended immediate surgery. She was aghast at this defect in her body. The next day she consulted another doctor who verified the diagnosis and recommendation. She scheduled the surgery for a few days later.

The very next morning, she found her car vandalized! She reported it to the police and then to her insurance company. To her horror, the insurance agent said her policy had lapsed. She had recently moved, and apparently the renewal notice from the company had not been forwarded.

She called the agent who had written the policy in her home town. He said the company should have notified him if the policy was about to lapse. No one had notified him, so the company was partly to blame for the lapse. He thought they would pay for the repairs.

When Helen told me all of this, I thought to myself, "Here is a person who has been one-down in relation to life for years. There is probably some part of her that experiences these misfortunes as confirming that she is no good. If I console her, not only will my words sound trivial, I will also be reinforcing her stance as victim."

So I told her, "You know, if this kind of thing *had to happen* to somebody, I am glad it happened to you instead of anyone else I know."

I paused to let the shock of this comment sink in. I then went on to say, "Your doctor discovered a lump in your breast and recommended surgery. Instead of meekly acquiescing to that recommendation, you took the initiative to contact a second doctor to get a second opinion. When it was assured that surgery was indicated, you immediately scheduled it.

"When you were told that your car insurance had lapsed, you didn't meekly acquiesce to that. You took the initiative to call your home agent to try to get that decision rescinded. You did exactly the right things to cope with some horrible situations. Most of the other people I know — probably including me — would not have had the initiative to deal with this kind of thing as assertively as you did. So if it had to happen to someone, I'm glad it happened to someone who could handle it so well."

H. Close. *The Journal of Pastoral Care,* Fall, 1992. Used with permission of the publisher.

Creating Metaphors

*If a story is worth telling,
it is worth improving upon.*

A number of people have asked me how to create metaphors. Here are a few suggestions.

Read. There are many folk tales, rabbinic stories, fairy tales and nursery stories that can be used therapeutically. Clinical vignettes from other therapists are often very powerful interventions. As you saturate your mind with examples, you create a mind-set for crafting your own. That is one reason why I have given so many examples in this book. Many of the clinical studies from Milton Erickson's work have a very beautiful and effective metaphoric quality to them.

Observe. Many processes in the world of nature are parallel to processes of healing and growth. Some are described in this book. To cultivate a sense of curiosity about nature and about life is not only personally enriching, but can also be the source of many therapeutic metaphors. Write out in detail some of the things you know about trees, weather patterns, the molting processes of crabs and lobsters, the ways the body heals itself, patterns on flowers and animals, the flight of insects and birds. What can you learn from a visit to the zoo? Or to a botanical garden? How does a sailboat sail? How does it right itself if capsized in a storm?

Milton Erickson sometimes instructed people to climb a mountain or visit a botanical garden. He once took a very depressed woman on an imaginary trip to the ocean just as a storm was subsiding, and talked with her about the storm and about life in the ocean. He then took her to the zoo, and then to an arboretum.[1]

There are other processes having to do with our own growth. How did we learn to walk? Or to write? Or to ride a bicycle? Or to swim? Reading in the fields of science, anthropology, history, and ecology will provide many useful metaphors.

You can observe other people also: children, people in a checkout line, rude drivers, people competing in sports, hikers.

Personal Experiences. I recently undertook what was for me a very strenuous hike up Angel's Landing in Zion National Park. The last few hundred yards were rather hazardous, and to me, totally intimidating. I knew I could never make it to the top. But I saw a spot about twenty yards ahead that I could make. When I got there, I saw another, and then another. In this way, I made it to the top rather easily. When I returned home, I wrote up this experience, and have used it with certain clients.

Remember things you have done with clients that seem to have been effective, or things they have said or done that have gained your attention. When you are absolutely sure you have totally disguised the participants and the setting, tell other clients or colleagues what you have observed.

Reflect. Write out in detail things you experience in your own living. Many of them will be valuable resources.

A chronically depressed man was thinking of living with his mother to shepherd her through the final years of her life. But well-meaning friends told him this was extremely unhealthy. Part of Martin's pathology is that he takes other people's advice much too seriously. So, of course, he asked my advice. If I told him I thought it was all right, I would simply be one more advice-giver, competing with the others. I would also implicitly be telling him that other people's advice was important.

So I told Martin of my moving to Florida several years ago. I chose to live with my father, as he was approaching his final days. At the end of our first year together, when he left for his summer vacation, he told me this had been the happiest year of his life. I told Martin, "I don't know if it was healthy or not for me to have lived with him, but I wouldn't take anything for that experience."

Share. Get together on a regular basis with a colleague or two to practice. One of you can describe a clinical situation. The other(s) can then create some kind of relevant story, maybe a personal experience, an allegory from nature, a report of another person's experience, or nursery story.

Such conscious activities will be deliberately programming your mind to be alert to this kind of thing. You will not only have more resources to draw from, but you will help build the cognitive processes that can create them.

Write. When you put things in writing, you give attention to your choice of words and phrases. Eventually, this craft will become ingrained, and you will tell your stories more easily and spontaneously.

When you write out things you have told clients, write them as though you *actually* said the things you *wish* you had said — as I have done in this book.

Remember, too, there is something of the showoff in all of us. When we share our creations with our friends and receive their affirmation, that's a wonderful stimulus to create more and better interventions.

When you have a few stories you have used successfully, try to find someplace to publish them. Unfortunately, that may not be easy. I don't know of any therapy journals that have a section for clinical vignettes. Newsletters from various organizations (such as the Milton Erickson Foundation, 3606 N. 24 St., Phoenix, AZ 85106-6500) sometimes publish vignettes. But most professional journals do not. Journals require that you surround your stories with a lot of theory. The theories then "justify" the stories. Maybe someday a journal will appear that will publish just the stories and let them stand on their own merit. If such a journal now exists, I am not aware of it.

When telling stories to clients, I do not introduce theory by interpreting the stories. That would be like interpreting a lullaby to a child. The client's subconscious mind can do the interpreting and applying much better than I can. The power of a metaphor is inherent; to explain it may dilute this power.

Putting the Pieces Together

Two incidents pull together some of the principles described in this book (reframing, metaphor, symmetry, Utopianism, utilization, drama and manipulation).

❖   ❖   ❖   ❖   ❖

A twenty-three-year-old graduate student consulted me for a variety of personal problems. The most pressing was her panic about speaking in public. The class she was now taking included an obligatory report to the entire class in about four weeks. Alice was terrified at the prospect.

In the course of our conversation, she said that she was the older sister of two younger brothers she had helped raise. Her three serious relationships had been with men who had more than their share of problems, and the relationships ended badly. She seemed to attract this kind of man, who in turn was the kind of man attracted to her. She could always see something good in them and felt she could bring it out, but she ended up feeling like a caretaker and felt used and disappointed.

She described her parents as extremely nice, good, quiet people, low-key and stable. She talked about a few other concerns, especially about her fear of becoming obese (she seemed almost underweight to me, and I was concerned about possible anorexia). She then returned to her concern about the oral report. She felt she was always on trial. If she did not do well, she would be severely judged and criticized.

I told her she was in good company with that kind of anxiety. Enrico Caruso, the famous singer, used to pace back and forth in the wings before he went on stage, often going to the bathroom several times. But once he got on stage and sang his first note, he was fine. It was like the pacing and the visits to the bathroom allowed him to build up emotional intensity. When he sang, it was then with enthusiasm and vitality. He didn't just stroll out and start half-heartedly singing. He had built up a store of energy to give life to his performance. He probably wouldn't have done as well if he had not been anxious beforehand.

I then mentioned an incident in my own life. I was preaching in a small church in south Florida. The regular minister was a large man, who was quite uncomfortable with the Florida heat. He had the air conditioner vent directed right at the pulpit, with maximum force. When I began my sermon, I placed my text on the pulpit and started to speak. My body was shielding the pulpit from the air conditioner.

After a couple of minutes, I stepped back for a moment to make a point, and a ferocious gust of wind from the air conditioner swept over the pulpit. As my notes started to blow away I slammed my hand down and managed to rescue all of the text except one page. There to my horror, all the most profound thoughts, expressed in the most beautiful language I had ever created fluttered meaninglessly to the floor.

Alice and I laughed heartily.

I then asked her if she were planning to have children. She said yes. I asked her if she were already beginning her scrap book of embarrassing stories to tell her children. She said she had a few stories but hadn't thought of them as a collection. I then asked her if her mother and dad told her of embarrassing incidents from their growing-up days.

She related a story her mother had told her about her high school prom. While she and her date were dancing blissfully, he stepped on the hem of her dress, which proceeded to rip all the way to the waist as they both fell to the floor. Alice said she remembered that story with special warmth. I told her she needed to have lots of stories like that out of her own life to tell her children. I thought the classroom report would be an excellent place to begin.

I then told her another story from my experience. I was riding home from high school on my bicycle — nobody had cars back then. As I was crossing the railroad tracks, a school bus loaded with my classmates was passing beside me. I decided to show off what a good bicycle rider I was. I yanked up on the handlebars so the bump on the front wheel would be smoothed out as it crossed the railroad tracks.

Something went wrong, and the front wheel froze, sending me and the bicycle sprawling spectacularly in the street in the presence of my friends.

Alice and I both laughed again. She said she didn't know why, but she loved hearing these stories.

I told her she needed to begin planning about how she could use her phobia of public speaking to her advantage. I pointed out that if she did poorly in the presentation, she might begin to get herself off her pedestal. I thought it was time she ceased making such unrealistic demands for perfection on herself. I reminded her that the kind of men who were attracted to her were attracted to her perfection. When she could mess up a little bit, she would get off the pedestal in their eyes too. Then she could begin to attract men who were normal.

I then told her that she ought to build some deliberate mistakes into her report. She could "mis-pronounciate" some words. She could make sure she "ain't done got the right grammar" all the time. She could put the "em-*phasis*" on the wrong "syll-*able*" on certain words. She could stumble over her place in the report. But it was essential that she practice these things, so they didn't sound deliberate. For them to be effective, it has to sound accidental.

I even proposed that she think about stumbling and falling on her way to the podium. But if she were to do that, I thought she would need a little more padding on her body because she was too skinny. She probably needed to gain at least five or six pounds of padding to cushion herself for the fall.

When I saw her the next week, she said she was already planning on how she could make some deliberate mistakes, such as dropping her charts and mispronouncing some words. The anxiety about her report was gone.

I was hiking with my daughter and her kids recently when six-year-old Geri started shrieking in terror: a bug had landed on the sleeve of her sweater! I grabbed her arm next to the bug and gently nudged it onto the back of my hand. As it crawled across my hand, I shook my finger at it angrily.

"You're a bad bug for scaring Geri. If you ever scare her again, I'm going to tell your Mommy on you, and you'll really be in trouble then."

The bug cooperated wonderfully by flying away at that precise moment.

Geri watched with rapt attention but was still somewhat shaken. So I said to her, "That was a bad bug to scare you wasn't it?" She agreed heartily. I then suggested that maybe we could find some other bugs and just *pretend* to be scared of them.

After failing to catch butterflies, anoles and water bugs, I finally dug around in the leaf humus and found a beetle. As it started crawling on my hand, I said, "Okay, let's all pretend to be scared of it. Let's all yell together." I started by screaming, "It's going to bite me, it's going to eat up my whole hand, it's going to eat up the whole world! Help! Eek!"

Geri and her mother playfully joined in pretending to be scared.

I then pointed out how interesting it looked — how different its legs looked from ours, how it walked and so forth.

We then found another bug I didn't recognize. I told her we could pretend to be scared of it without picking it up, since it might actually sting a little. Then we found a grandaddy longlegs. It wasn't full grown, so we labeled it a daddy longlegs. As it was climbing on my hand, I asked Geri what we should name it.

"Climby."

I asked whimsically, "I wonder if Climby might like to have a small hand to climb on."

Within a few minutes Geri was giggling as Climby walked all over her hand.

I then told her a story about a mommy and daddy who were out walking with their two little children, Alicia (Geri's favorite name) and Brutus. Daddy had found a bird feather on the ground and showed it to Alicia. He had her smell it, feel how soft it was when she rubbed it on her nose and how easily it bent in her hand. Then he gave it to Brutus, who grabbed it and started chasing Alicia, crying, "I'm going to touch you with this bird feather! I'm going to touch you with this feather!"

"Do you know what happened? Alicia was scared to death! She started screaming and running and crying, and wanted Daddy to pick her up and hold her and keep that terrible bird feather away from her."

I then asked Geri if she thought Alicia was really scared of the bird feather.

"No."

"What do you think she was really scared of?"

"Her brother, who was being mean to her."

I agreed, and we then looked for some more bugs as we continued our walk.

There are probably several possible understandings about why this was an effective intervention. I was aware of four principles. I wanted to acknowledge her fright, but without suggesting there was any real danger. I wanted, through the playfulness and exaggeration, to imply that the bug was harmless. I wanted to give her a sense of control (deliberately looking for bugs to be scared of and then giving "Climby" a name). Finally I told the story in order to normalize the whole situation and to reinforce her new attitude about bugs.

Geri called me two days later to tell me about another "Climby" she had seen at her home.

"Did you pretend to be scared of him?"

"NO!"

We then talked some more about "Climby #2." I told her when she saw him again to say "Hello" for me.

H. Close, "Symptom Prescription in a Case of Pediatric Phobia," originally published in the *Georgia Association for Marriage and Family Therapy Newsletter,* Summer, 1992. Used with permission of the publisher.

26 ❖

Ping
Ancient Art Becomes Contemporary Therapy

The controversy still rages. Is PING really a radical new discovery, or is it merely the rediscovery and restatement of principles of life well known to the ancients? Perhaps there is truth on both sides of the question. Doubtless the ancients knew of PING — we see glimpses of it still in many community dances and purification rites. But whether any of them ever grasped its full significance for psychotherapy and personal growth is doubtful. Perhaps only the aborigines of Australia, living so intimately with marsupials, maintained the practice intact throughout the ages.

It is still too early to tell whether PING will take its rightful place among the therapies, or whether it will be dismissed as being superficial. Many good therapies have taken the country by storm for a while. They would accomplish things never before believed possible, only to fade into obscurity within a few years. Let us hope that PING suffers no such ignominious fate. At this point it does not seem likely.

If PING does eventually suffer discredit, it will probably be due to the multitude of PING centers that are springing [sic] up everywhere. Many are staffed by well-meaning but inadequately trained therapists. Some have no doubt attracted charlatans, hoping for personal gain by exploiting other people's sufferings.

For those of you not yet familiar with PING, let me outline what I consider to be the essentials. PING is a specific therapy, to be employed wisely and to be carefully integrated into the total fabric of a person's life. In its essence it is this: *Once every day, in some public place, with absolute seriousness, one should hop instead of walk!*

PING, of course, takes its name from the last syllable of the word HOPPING. It was applied at first to only a few kinds of pathological conditions: depression, inhibitions, insomnia, over-concern for one's public image, etc. Its usefulness in treating other conditions soon became apparent: hyperactivity, anorexia, impotence and others. Even exhibitionism, for which at first PING might seem to be contraindicated, has responded well. Students are now working on ways to apply some of the more advanced principles of PING to schizophrenia. But at this point the results are inconclusive.

To the best of my knowledge, there are only two offshoots from the mainstream: the ultra-radical GING (from SPRINGING) and the ultra-conservative TING (from HESITATING), which considers even PING to be too radical. GING advocates insist on the flamboyant and dramatic, saying that you must leap, spring, jump, making each movement into a work of art. TING advocates, on the other hand, think it is enough if one merely hesitates a fraction of a second after each step. Ah well, perhaps it is one's fate to see one's work corrupted by revisionists.

So far only two professional organizations have arisen: PING (PING Institute for Normal Growth) and HOPPING (Happy Order of PINGING People's Inter-National Group). No doubt there will be a demand from one of these groups for licensing procedures. This will probably come from PING, the more responsible of the two groups. Requirements will undoubtedly include intensive experience as a patient in both individual and group settings, plus academic instruction and a period of supervision.

It is my conviction that experience as a patient is mandatory. How can you lead other people into the depths and heights (I'm speaking symbolically now, not referring to how low you crouch in a PING, or how high you jump) of an experience unless you have been there yourself? People need to learn this kind of thing from a patient, loving therapist who will not exploit their vulnerability. Most practitioners are agreed that PING should first be learned on a one-to-one basis, in the sanctity of a therapist's office. Then the person can meaningfully participate in a group experience or an intensive workshop.

The workshops are interesting. They usually begin with a series of testimonials about the value of PING, along with a desire to learn more and to find the dedication to practice PING unashamedly before one's friends.

From the very beginning of the rediscovery of PING, there have been elaborations. Couples PING involves a husband and wife in therapy together, and of course Family PING involves the whole family. It is understood now that the presuppositions underlying Couples PING and Family PING are quite different from those underlying the practice of Individual PING. Some day, however, there will probably be a researcher who will discover that underlying these apparent differences are certain realities common to both. But at this point, people are insisting on additional training for Couples PING and for Family PING.

Some of the elaborations on Individual PING are impressive in and of themselves. Standard PING is a normal hop, both feet loosely together. Petite PING is a series of very short hops, with ankles and knees together. Butterfly PING is a hop in which the feet are separated momentarily when in the air and brought back together before they touch the floor.

In Zigzag PING (ZING), the torso moves in a straight line, but the feet make a kind of zigzag motion across the floor. Semi-PING is hopping on just one foot and is regarded by many as a good way to begin. It gives the impression that something is wrong with the other foot. Purists, of course, reject this as being deceptive and therefore counterproductive.

Semi-PING has been given a few other names by those obsessed with such things. Mono-pedal PING is the true generic name, while Dextro-pedal PING and Sinistro-pedal PING represent hopping on the right or the left foot respectively. Symmetrical PING is hopping first with one foot and then the other, while asymmetrical PING is hopping on only one foot. Symmetrical PING is very much akin to skipping (KING for short).

I have already alluded to the existence of Couples PING, Family PING and Group PING. Many couples have commented on what a tremendous new experience it was when, for the first time, they PINGED into the bedroom! PINGING in place has value for the person just beginning to learn the basics. Primal PING and TP (Transcendental PING) are for the more advanced.

In closing, let me give you my own testimonial. I was embarrassed at first by the very idea of hopping in public. I could see no value in something that looked so irrelevant and . . . well, frankly, absurd. But my wife insisted that we needed to do something to rejuvenate our marriage. So with great hesitancy we consulted the PING therapist together.

Remember, we were both very proper people, carefully schooled in the proprieties of our culture. You can imagine our reaction when Dr. K. nonchalantly PINGED into the waiting room and introduced himself to us. When I later mentioned my shock to the friend who had referred us, he said that when Dr. K. received his doctorate, he PINGED across the platform to be awarded the degree. The impact was stunning! Well, it was no less so there in the waiting room.

However, we stuck it out and patiently learned the principles. He slowly and patiently led us back to the basics and then nurtured our growth together. There's just no way I can tell you of the new sense of freedom and elation you will feel once you get over your initial hesitancy. Old habits and patterns vanish. Problems that were once overwhelming now seem trivial. Social conventions that were once enslaving simply vanish. We have a new outlook on life, a new acceptance, a new joy. I don't mean to say that we have "arrived," but PING has opened doors for us we never knew existed. We heartily recommend it to you.

PING!

Bibliography

American Journal of Psychotherapy, Vol. 51, #2.(Spring, 1997) "The Use of Metaphor by an Artless First-Time Psychotherapist," Joanne Sinai, M.D.

Bateson, G. (1985) *Steps to an Ecology of Mind.* New York: Ballantine Books.

Bateson, G. (1958) *Naven: A Survey of The Problems Suggested by a Composite Picture of The Culture of a New Guinea Tribe Drawn from Three Points of View,* 3rd Ed. Stanford, CA: Stanford University Press.

Bateson, M.C. (1984) *With a Daughter's Eye.* New York: William Morrow & Co., Inc.

Close, H. "Pastoral Care for an Unconscious Person," *The Journal of Pastoral Care* (Summer, 1998) Relevant to the material on fantasy.

Erickson, M.H. (1980) E. Rossi (ed.) *Innovative Hypnotherapy,* Vol. IV. New York: Irvington Publishers, Inc.

Erickson, M.H. (1989) *The Wisdom of Milton H. Erickson.* New York: Paragon House: Irvington Publishers, Inc.

Erickson, M.H. (1982) *My Voice Will Go With You.* New York: W.W. Norton & Co., Inc.

Erickson, M.H. (1980) E. Rossi (ed.) *The Collected Papers of Milton H. Erickson on Hypnosis,* Vol. IV. New York: Irvington Publishers, Inc.

Erickson, M.H. (1980) Edited with commentary by Jeffrey Zeig. *A Teaching Seminar with Milton H. Erickson.* New York: Brunner/Mazel, Inc.

Gardner, R. (1972) *Therapeutic Communication with Children: The Mutual Storytelling Technique.* Northvale, New Jersey: Jason Aronson.

Haley, J. (1963) *Strategies of Psychotherapy.* New York: Grune & Stratton.

Haley, J. (1976) *Problem-Solving Therapy.* San Francisco: Jossey-Bass, Inc., Publishers.

Haley, J. (1973) *Uncommon Therapy.* New York: W.W. Norton & Co., Inc.

Ingram, J. L. (1994) "The Role of Figurative Language in Psychotherapy: A Methodological Examination," *Metaphor and Symbolic Activity* 9 (4), 271-288. Lawrence Erlbaum Associates, Inc.

Jeffrey, M. J. (1997) *Restructuring Personality Disorder.* New York: The Guilford Press.

King, M.L. (1981) *Strength to Love.* Minneapolis: Augsburg Fortress Publishers.

Napier, A. and A. Whitaker (1978) *The Family Crucible.* New York: Harper & Row.

Siegelman, E.Y. (1990) *Metaphor and Meaning in Psychotherapy.* New York: The Guilford Press.

Tillich, P. (1952) *The Courage to Be.* New Haven: Yale University Press.

Whitaker, C.A. and W.M. Bumrry (1988) *Dancing With the Family: A Symbolic-Experiential Approach.* New York: Brunner/Mazel, Inc.

Watzlawick, P. and R. Fisch (1974) *Change: Principles of Problem Formulation and Problem Resolution.* New York: W.W. Norton & Co., Inc.

Watzlawick, P., J. Bevin and D. Jackson (1967) *Pragmatics of Human Communication.* New York: W.W. Norton & Co., Inc.

Whitaker, C.A. (1989) *Midnight Musings of a Family Therapist.* New York: W.W. Norton & Co., Inc.

White, Michael and D. Epston (1990) *Narrative Means to Therapeutic Ends.* New York: W.W. Norton & Co., Inc.

Zeig, J. (ed.) (1994) *Ericksonian Methods: The Essence of the Story* (edited proceedings of the fifth International Erickson Congress). New York: Brunner/Mazel Publishers, Inc.

Zeig, J. (1985) *Experiencing Erickson: An Introduction to the Man and His Work*. New York: Brunner/Mazel, Inc.

Permissions

Excerpts from the following publications were used with permission:

Chapter 10: The Heart and the Mind
Tolstoy, L. (1960) *The Death of Ivan Ilych and Other Stories,* Chapter VI, p. 131f. Translated by Aylmer Maude. New York: Signet Classics, Oxford University Press.

Chapter 11: World View
Rosenhan, D. (1973) *Science,* 179 (January 1973, pp. 250-258).

Chapter 16: Utilization
Nichols, B. (1972) *Father Figure.* William Heinemann Limited and Eric Glass Limited.

Newsletter of the Milton H. Erickson Foundation (Spring, 1994).

Chapter 17: Metaphor and Reframing
Clark, M. (1956) *Captain's Bride, General's Lady.* New York: McGraw-Hill Inc.
"Wayne" was General Mark W. Clark, who led the American campaign in Italy.

Chapter 19: Metaphor and Rapport
Haley, J. (1973) *Uncommon Therapy: The Psychiatric Techniques of Milton H. Erickson.* New York: W.W. Norton & Co., Inc.

301

Dyess, W.E. (1944) *The Dyess Story.* New York: G.P. Putnam Sons. This account was not published until January, 1994, for fear of reprisals against other prisoners. It appeared first in newspapers. The book came out just a month before Colonel Dyess was killed in a plane crash in California.

Newsletter of The Georgia Association for Marriage and Family Therapy (Winter 1992).

Chapter 20: Drama as Metaphor
Erickson, M.H. (1980) E. Rossi (ed.) *The Collected Papers of Milton H. Erickson on Hypnosis,* Vol. IV. New York: Irvington Publishers, Inc.

Psychotherapy: Theory, Research and Practice (January, 1974).

Chapter 26: PING
Pilgrimage. (Spring, 1973).

Index

MORE BOOKS WITH *IMPACT*

We think you will find these Impact Publishers titles of interest:

THE 60-SECOND SHRINK
101 Strategies for Staying Sane in a Crazy World
Arnold A. Lazarus, Ph.D., and Clifford N. Lazarus, Ph.D.
Softcover: $12.95   176pp.   ISBN: 1-886230-04-8
Over 100 mental health "morsels," each can be read in about
a minute — provides common-sense solutions to a wide
variety of problems.

MASTER YOUR PANIC & TAKE BACK YOUR LIFE
Twelve Treatment Sessions to Overcome
High Anxiety (2nd Edition)
Denise F. Beckfield, Ph.D.
Softcover: $14.95   304pp.   ISBN: 1-886230-08-0
Help for the 24 million adult Americans who suffer
from high anxiety. Proven, research-based methods in
a comprehensive anxiety treatment program.

YOU CAN BEAT DEPRESSION
A Guide to Prevention and Recovery (2nd Edition)
John Preston, Psy.D.
Softcover: $11.95   176pp.   ISBN: 1-886230-02-1
The most readable book on depression, with proven
strategies for self-help — and how to get good profes-
sional help when needed. Information on latest drug
therapies and other methods of treatment.

YOUR PERFECT RIGHT
A Guide to Assertive Living (7th Edition)
Robert E. Alberti, Ph.D., and Michael L. Emmons, Ph.D.
Softcover: $12.95   Hardcover: $17.95   256pp.
Twenty-fifth Anniversary Edition of the assertiveness
book most recommended by psychologists — fifth
most recommended among all self-help books!

Ask your local bookseller, or write for our free catalog.
Prices effective October 1, 1998, and subject to change without notice.

Impact 📚 Publishers®
POST OFFICE BOX 910
SAN LUIS OBISPO, CALIFORNIA 93406